mafiaboy

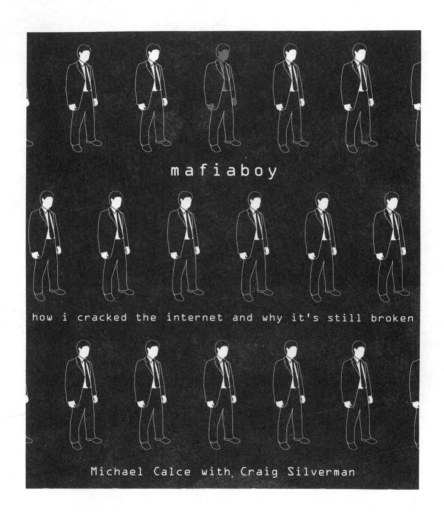

m a f i a b o y

how i cracked the internet and why it's still broken

Michael Calce with Craig Silverman

VIKING
CANADA

VIKING CANADA

Published by the Penguin Group

Penguin Group (Canada), 90 Eglinton Avenue East, Suite 700,
Toronto, Ontario, Canada M4P 2Y3
(a division of Pearson Canada Inc.)

Penguin Group (USA) Inc., 375 Hudson Street, New York, New York 10014, U.S.A.
Penguin Books Ltd, 80 Strand, London WC2R 0RL, England
Penguin Ireland, 25 St Stephen's Green, Dublin 2, Ireland
(a division of Penguin Books Ltd)
Penguin Group (Australia), 250 Camberwell Road, Camberwell, Victoria 3124, Australia
(a division of Pearson Australia Group Pty Ltd)
Penguin Books India Pvt Ltd, 11 Community Centre, Panchsheel Park,
New Delhi – 110 017, India
Penguin Group (NZ), 67 Apollo Drive, Rosedale, North Shore 0745,
Auckland, New Zealand (a division of Pearson New Zealand Ltd)
Penguin Books (South Africa) (Pty) Ltd, 24 Sturdee Avenue, Rosebank,
Johannesburg 2196, South Africa

Penguin Books Ltd, Registered Offices: 80 Strand, London WC2R 0RL, England

First published 2008

1 2 3 4 5 6 7 8 9 10 (RRD)

Copyright © Michael Calce and Craig Silverman, 2008

LIBRARY AND ARCHIVES CANADA CATALOGUING IN PUBLICATION

Calce, Michael
Mafiaboy : how I cracked the Internet and why it's still broken / Michael
Calce, Craig Silverman.

ISBN 978-0-670-06748-0

1. Calce, Michael.   2. Computer crimes.   3. Computer security.   4. Computer
hackers—Canada—Biography.   I. Silverman, Craig   II. Title.

HV6773.C34 2008   364.16'8092   C2008-902735-3

Visit the Penguin Group (Canada) website at **www.penguin.ca**

Special and corporate bulk purchase rates available; please see
www.penguin.ca/corporatesales or call 1-800-810-3104, ext. 477 or 474

In loving memory of Nicholas Groner
(August 24, 1984-February 17, 1997)

You will never be forgotten

Contents

I think it's fair to say that personal computers have become the most empowering tool we've ever created. They're tools of communication, they're tools of creativity, and they can be shaped by their user.

—Bill Gates

"HOT ON THE TRAIL OF 'MAFIABOY'" read a headline on technology news site Wired.com on February 15, 2000. That was the day Mafiaboy, my online alter ego, became a household name.

Before that moment, I was just an ordinary kid growing up in a Montreal suburb. I hung out with friends, went to school, and played basketball. I was a fifteen-year-old grade ten student living in my father's house. Then I suddenly became international news.

In February 2000, the FBI named me, Mafiaboy, as a suspect in a series of online attacks that had targeted some of the giants of the internet, including Yahoo.com, eBay.com, CNN.com, and E*TRADE.com. Their websites had been slowed or had completely ground to a halt as a result of massive denial-of-service (DoS) attacks. Just like you would jam a phone system with a barrage of calls to prevent anyone else from getting through, someone had bombarded their web servers with so many requests that they were unable to serve content to visitors.

That someone was me.

Working from my bedroom on a suburban street in Montreal, I launched what remains one of the biggest series of DoS attacks ever to hit the internet. As a result, Mafiaboy became famous. Infamous. My online alias was mentioned on the news in countries around the world. Then U.S. president Bill Clinton responded to the attacks by convening a cybersecurity summit at the White House. Janet Reno, his attorney general, said her office wouldn't rest until I was apprehended.

I was hunted by the FBI and RCMP and eventually arrested and charged with close to seventy counts related to computer crimes. Along the way, my father was arrested on a questionable charge that was later dropped. A court order prevented me from seeing my best friends and from using computers and the internet. Reporters camped outside my home and school.

My life fell apart. I lost a sense of who I was.

This had never been a problem for me before. Ever since I first laid hands on a PC, at six years old, I knew my life would be forever linked to computers. School could be a struggle, but the computer always made sense to me. It was as if using it was encoded in my DNA. I soon moved from playing games to going online and learning about computer programming and networking. I was then drawn to the darker corners of the internet, joining hacker groups and learning how to inflict damage on my online enemies. Computers and hacking became my life. Then they forever changed it.

My attacks of 2000 were illegal, reckless, and, in many ways, simply stupid. At the time I didn't realize the consequences of what I was doing. That doesn't excuse what I did. It's important for me to state clearly that I recognize and regret the damage I caused. This book is not meant to excuse or glorify what I did. It is the story of how a child's obsession with computers resulted in some of the most written-about online attacks in history.

Despite entreaties from the press over the last eight years, I have kept quiet about what really happened on the night of my arrest, and about the events that followed. I remained silent as the media and law enforcement painted a portrait of me that is still held to be the truth to this day. I want to set straight the many inaccuracies about me that persist. I have done my best to verify my own memory of events with court records, evidence, and other sources. I have also attempted to speak with people who were involved in my case but have been largely rebuffed. In truth, they've already had their say. Now it's my turn.

Aside from a personal desire to open up about my life as Mafiaboy, there is another, more urgent, reason why my story now needs to be told. It has taken years for me to come to terms with my crimes and to gain a new level of perspective and maturity. During this period, I have watched the internet grow less secure, more dangerous, and frighteningly criminal. The average computer user is increasingly becoming victim to online fraud, identity theft, extortion, and other serious crimes. Technology companies continue to earn profits, but the average user is overwhelmed with spam, worms, viruses, and other threats. This wasn't the way the internet was supposed to work. I believe I can play a role in helping raise awareness about online security, and teach average users how they can protect themselves.

My journey to this book began a few years ago when I started writing a computer security column for *Le Journal de Montréal,* a French-language newspaper. I focused on basic user security and worked hard to try to educate people about how they can protect themselves. But eventually I realized the best way to have an impact is to share my experience and show how it relates to our current, worrisome situation. This is the story of Mafiaboy, but it is also a warning about today's insecure online world.

As Bill Gates expressed in his famous quote, personal computers are incredibly empowering because they can be shaped by their user. Personal computers and the internet offer unlimited potential for creativity, personal expression, and communication. Even in a time of constant online threats, the average user still has the power to control and shape his or her computer and internet experience. We have the means to protect ourselves. The problem is that too many people are unaware of how to take online security into their own hands.

By each doing our part, we can make the internet safer and more secure, and help defeat the next generation of misguided Mafiaboys.

PART 1

Mafiaboy 1.0

CHAPTER ONE

Raid at Rue du Golf

IT WAS SUPPOSED TO BE ONE OF THE BEST DAYS of Tommy's life. He had received the call: Tommy was going to be a made man. His friends were excited, and even his mom was thrilled. She couldn't help but fix his shirt collar and give him a kiss before he headed out, wearing one of his best suits.

"Listen," she told him, "you be careful. I wish you lots of luck. I love you."

I remember watching him walk through the door into a wood-panelled room expecting to see a gathering of his new mob family. But the room was empty. Tommy got what was coming to him—a bullet in the back of the head.

He should've known it was going to happen. Tommy had broken the rules and beaten a made guy to death. But they came and got him at a time he least expected, and so his last moments on earth were a combination of total joy, surprise, fright, and then ... nothing.

GOODFELLAS IS ONE OF MY FAVOURITE FILMS. Joe Pesci's performance as the ultra-violent Tommy DeVito has always stuck with me. It was a great role in a great film, but I remember it because my life changed dramatically at the exact same time as Tommy's.

On a Friday night in April 2000 I was watching *Goodfellas* while staying over at my friend Patrick's house, a beautiful home in the suburban West Island of Montreal. It was around 3 A.M. and we were just two fifteen-year-old kids staying up late, eating junk food, and watching a really violent movie. Like Tommy as he headed out to get made, I thought everything was right with the world.

As we watched Tommy primping for his big day, my cellphone rang. Who could be calling me so late? I picked up the phone, thinking it was an ex-girlfriend or a friend wanting to meet up—I was known to stay up late on the weekend. In fact, I had for years been staying up late just about every night. But hardly any of my friends knew the schedule I had been keeping on weeknights: home from school and right to the computer until early in the morning. I'd break for dinner, but that was about it.

I was living a huge portion of my life online, interacting with a whole other universe of people, and taking part in activities that my friends and family wouldn't have understood even if I'd sat them down and explained it all bit by bit. It had been my secret until recent events made me fearful of being exposed. But just hanging out with my best friend watching a movie I felt relaxed. I was lost in the story. Until my phone rang.

The display showed that the call was coming from my home. This was strange, but I thought maybe it was my older brother, Lorenzo, calling to see where I was. I wasn't even close. It was my father on the line.

"Hi, Michael," he said. "Where are you?"

My dad's voice sounded as if he'd had the wind knocked out of him. It was very late and he already knew where I was. Something must be wrong.

"Um, I'm where I told you I would be—at Patrick's house," I said. "Why?"

"They're here, Michael," he told me.

"It's 3 A.M., Dad. What are you talking about? Who's there?"

But I knew who was there. I could sense whom he was talking about just by the tone of his voice. After months of evasive manoeuvres on my part, the police had finally made a move. They were at my house, with my family. Yet here I was, sitting in Patrick's house, watching a movie. It seemed strange—and wrong.

"The RCMP are here, and they're looking for you," my father told me. "They said they are coming to pick you up. Wait at the corner of Patrick's street for them."

"What's going to happen, Dad? Are you coming along?" I asked him, not understanding if I was being arrested or if the RCMP were picking me up for questioning. Who just goes out and waits on a street corner for the cops? I was scared and confused. This wasn't the way I pictured it happening, with me separated from my family.

"No, they are arresting me for unrelated charges, but they have to bring you home to read you your rights, so I contacted the lawyer," he told me.

I couldn't understand why he was being taken away. It also didn't make sense that I would be picked up and then brought home just to be read my rights. But my dad didn't have any more information to share with me.

"Don't worry, everything will be fine," he told me.

"All right, Dad, hang in there," I told him. "I will fix it."

I had no idea what I was going to do. I ended the call and looked over to see Patrick staring at me in disbelief.

"What the hell is going on? You look like a ghost!" he said.

"Sorry, bro," I told him. "Something happened. I have to go. I'll explain later."

On the TV screen, Tommy was lying on the floor in a pool of blood.

A FEW MINUTES LATER, I was waiting at the end of Patrick's street for the police. I didn't know if it was part of the police's strategy to have me standing alone on a dark street corner with no one to comfort me or offer advice, but it was having an effect. I guess they knew I wouldn't run. I was fifteen years old. Where could I go? Nowhere. I stood there while my thoughts ran away with me.

The big houses were dark and it was just me, all alone, waiting to be arrested. I knew it was real, but a part of me kept thinking—hoping—it was a dream. Can this really be happening? I hoped to wake up soon and inhale a deep breath of relief. My pulse was steady, but my mind was racing. Had I taken care of everything? What was still in the house? Shit, think! My computers, what files did I still have on them? What do the cops know? What did they find at our house?

Two lights appeared down the street and a van emerged behind them in the darkness. The unmarked burgundy van came to a halt beside me and the side door slid open. I saw a group of police officers inside. A tall man with blondish hair stepped out. He was wearing a bulletproof vest.

"Michael, will you come with us, please," the man instructed in English with a French accent.

He was polite in his words and actions. Nobody came flying out of the van to grab me or wrestle me to the ground. No guns were drawn, and I wasn't put in handcuffs. But as I looked into the eyes of the man I would later come to know as Corporal Marc Gosselin of the Royal Canadian Mounted Police, one emotion was clear: satisfaction. He was happy to be leading me into that van. This late-night rendezvous on a quiet suburban street was for him the culmination of months of investigative work. He was enjoying the moment.

I, however, was willing myself to be calm. For the most part, it was working. I decided not to respond to him but made my way to the doors at the back of the van. I started thinking maybe they've got nothing and are just investigating. Then I recalled the phone conversation with my dad and understood I was being arrested.

Inside the van, I was surrounded by officers. One sat next to me, one sat directly in front of me, and two more were in the driver and passenger seats. Corporal Gosselin sat up front in the passenger seat.

"You know why you're here, right?" he asked.

Again I decided not to respond, but I did turn to him with a blank look on my face. I wasn't going to say anything. Every once in a while, Corporal Gosselin turned in his seat and looked at me, as though he were trying to get a read. I was doing my best not to show any emotion. The ride was mostly silent, but I kept thinking that my dad had been arrested and it was all my fault. I now knew he wouldn't be able to help me. I wanted him there. I knew he would be the best person to have around in this situation.

As we came down the main road that led to my house in Île Bizard, an island off the island of Montreal, I could see the street was dark except for a few street lamps. But my house was lit up as though a party was going on. There were several unmarked police cars and vans parked in front, but no officers in sight.

The van pulled into my driveway and an officer got out and opened the van's door for me. As I stepped out I immediately felt more comfortable. I was at home. I gave a sigh of relief as the officers led me to the partially open front door.

I walked inside my house and into the centre of a big police raid. Officers were everywhere, most of them examining or carting away electronics. And not just computers: It looked like they were searching or seizing anything that had a screen or was plugged into the wall. I saw officers in the living room, examining our satellite TV receiver. I looked up the front staircase to my bedroom and saw cops walking in and out. They were in every room I could see, and they were busy at work. A couple of them shot me glances when I walked in. Then they went back to work, examining, unplugging. I'm surprised they didn't take away our toaster.

I then saw my stepmother, Carole. She was dressed in a housecoat and moving around the house, frazzled and concerned. My father was nowhere to be seen: He had already been taken into custody.

Soon Lorenzo, coming home from a night out, burst through the door, bewildered as to what was going on. I was at the dining room table, surrounded by officers. My stepmother was on the phone in panic mode. And our house was filled with cops. Lorenzo was in total shock. He asked an officer what was going on and was directed to Corporal Gosselin, who explained they were there to arrest me.

I overheard an RCMP officer telling my stepmother that they would be questioning me at RCMP headquarters and that my lawyer could find me there. It dawned on me that the police had likely planned to arrest my father and me on the same day as a pressure tactic. They knew I would be more vulnerable without my dad there to help me. Or perhaps they wanted to conceal the fact that they were primarily investigating me. Weeks earlier, my lawyer had warned us to expect the unexpected. This was it.

With this in mind, I resolved not to break under pressure and to keep my mouth shut until my father, our lawyer, and I could talk things over. That was my mission for the night: I had to keep calm and stay quiet. Not an easy task for a fifteen year old in my situation.

An officer read me my rights and asked if I understood everything. I nodded, stood up, and was then arrested for the first time in my life. I was now officially in the custody of the RCMP. The officers seemed pleased as they led me outside. I was going downtown, literally, to RCMP headquarters in Westmount.

As they were taking me away my brother yelled to me in Italian, *"Non dire niente!"*

Don't say anything.

That's what I was telling myself over and over again.

An officer snapped at him and said not to speak to me, especially in a language they didn't understand. He said he'd arrest him as well if he continued doing it.

The police put me back in the van I had arrived in, and we began the forty-minute drive to headquarters. Images from every cop movie and TV show I had ever seen were running through my head. I began wondering what they would do to me at the police station.

With me now arrested and in custody, the officers in the van seemed to loosen up. As they talked among themselves, one person in particular caught my attention. While the other officers spoke in French, she spoke only in English, and it was clearly her mother tongue. And she wasn't in uniform, as many of the others were. I heard her say, "Everything is on the up and up."

For some reason, that made me suspect this was even bigger than I'd thought. She must be FBI. I hadn't seen any identification, but I felt sure. She was different from the others. She wasn't Canadian. She had to be FBI.

This told me a few things, none of them good. First, it meant that what I had done was serious enough that the FBI came to Canada to carry out a joint investigation. I also knew it meant it wouldn't be an easy court battle if both U.S. and Canadian law enforcement were involved. They were working together to get me.

I had read on the internet that something like fourteen computer crime units had been dispatched to locate me. I had seen stories about what I'd done in every major news source I could think of. I had watched CNN go on and on about me. But I was still surprised to be sitting near an FBI agent.

This set my imagination off again. The presence of the FBI meant that my case was an international incident. The Mounties may be known for always getting their man, but the FBI was known, to me at least, for being pretty ruthless once they got him. Based on the press coverage, I was the most famous computer hacker in the world. Now they had me, so what was next?

Île Bizard is connected to the island of Montreal via a bridge. Crossing that bridge meant I was no longer at home: I was on their turf. Even though I was under a huge amount of stress and dealing with an overwhelming sense of fear and panic, crossing that bridge gave me a moment of pure relief.

They had me, but I also knew what they didn't have.

JUST A FEW WEEKS EARLIER, I had stood on that bridge and looked down at the water. I knew that one day soon I might be arrested. I had known for weeks that the police were close to finding me, close to making their case. So late that night I took the keys to my dad's van and drove to the bridge with a very important item contained in plastic bags. I could feel the various parts moving around in the bags as I grabbed them from the van and walked along the bridge. What was once a solid computer hard drive located inside my PC was now smashed to bits thanks to the hammering job I'd done in the garage. For good measure, I had also covered it in magnets to help destroy the data and doused it with liquid. I needed to make sure no one could ever access the hard drive or the data on it. It was a smoking gun.

That bridge, and the water passing underneath it, represented the final part of my plan to cover my tracks. I slowly emptied the contents of the bags into the water, making sure to drop different parts into different places. Then I took the largest remaining piece and threw it as far as I could.

I watched it hit the surface and disappear under a series of ripples that barely disturbed the water. At that moment I felt safe. I also felt smart, like I had just given myself an advantage over my pursuers.

The water was calm. I stared at it for a bit and then drove home.

NOW, IN A VAN SURROUNDED BY COPS on our way to police headquarters, with my father in custody, my family in a panic, and my freedom taken away, I crossed that bridge into Montreal. I looked out the window at the water. It was tranquil and dark as it had been weeks before. I thought of what lay beneath the surface, the metal parts corroding and being swept up by the current and carried away. I knew the police would never find that critical piece of evidence.

A brief, imperceptible smile crossed my lips.

CHAPTER TWO

As Seen on CNN

WHAT HAD TAKEN THEM so long?

I couldn't help but wonder why, if so many law enforcement agencies were after me, the police hadn't come sooner. Within about a week of me causing the websites of CNN, Amazon, Yahoo!, eBay, and other internet giants to grind to a halt, my online alias was being reported in the press. They had moved surprisingly fast.

"The FBI sought to question several hackers Tuesday in its investigation into last week's attacks against major Web sites, looking for people known by their Internet screen names 'coolio,' 'mafiaboy,' and 'nachoman,'" reported the Associated Press on February 15, 2000.

Mafiaboy. It was a name I had chosen years before as my handle, the name I used in online chat rooms or when dealing with other hackers. Many hackers adopt an alias, and that's what I had chosen as mine. As stereotypical as it may seem for an Italian teenager to have adopted that name, it certainly sounded a whole lot better than "nachoman" when it started finding its way into the press in mid-February 2000.

February 15 was the day most people first heard the name Mafiaboy. That was the day U.S. president Bill Clinton convened a cybersecurity summit at the White House, and the FBI put out the word that it wanted to question me along with two other hackers. Our names dominated the headlines.

I was at my friend Brian's house, watching CNN. The anchor gave a brief summary of an upcoming story: The FBI had announced the names of three hackers it wanted to question in connection with the online attacks the week before. My stomach clenched, and I waited in suspense for the commercial break to be over. Finally, the news came back on, and my alias was indeed included among those wanted for questioning. I have to admit I was also excited, maybe even a little proud. I never expected to hear my handle broadcast on CNN, or to prompt the president of the United States to convene a summit with some of the country's top technology and computer-security leaders. And now the FBI wanted to find and question me.

I hadn't been paying much attention to the media at the time. I cared more about what was going on among the hackers I interacted with online. I cared what they thought, not what the press was saying. But that day, CNN broke the news right in front of my face and treated it as if a war had broken out. What had I done?

Brian knew a bit about computers, though he wasn't obsessed with them like I was. I don't know what came over me, but I decided I wanted to confide in him that I was Mafiaboy. Part of me wanted to see his reaction; part of me just needed to tell somebody my secret.

"You know those web attacks they're talking about on TV?" I asked him.

"Yeah."

"I did them."

There was no preamble. I just blurted it out. Brian was unfazed.

"Shut up," he said, not believing me. He thought I was messing with him.

We went back and forth, me insisting and him refusing to take me seriously. He knew I was into computers but had no idea how deep my interest went. After a few minutes he realized I was serious. Maybe it was the look in my eyes, or my insistence. But he finally believed me, though it seemed incredible. We joked about it at first, even though we both had a clear sense that the predicament I was in was really bad. Aside from maybe my brother, Brian was the only person in the world who knew for sure that Michael Calce was Mafiaboy and that I had orchestrated the web attacks. I knew that he could keep my secret, that he wouldn't rat me out—that was the least of my worries.

I realize now that part of me needed him to know. Everything about the attacks up to that point had existed online. I had performed them from behind a computer screen, and my few real discussions about them had taken place in online chats. The CNN story took it from the virtual world into the physical realm. This was real. I knew I would need those close to me to be on my side. More importantly, I realized I would need to tell someone else what I had done. I needed to tell my dad.

My stomach clenched again.

THE POLICE VAN turned into an underground parking garage at RCMP headquarters and came to a stop. We climbed out and the officers led me toward an elevator. I saw that the other vehicles in the garage were like the one I had just exited—unmarked and with civilian plates. Ghost cars.

We rode the elevator up a couple of floors. I felt anxious but was also fascinated by this personal tour of RCMP headquarters. We walked down an office-lined corridor, then stopped at a large door. Corporal Gosselin opened it for me. Inside was a conference room with a massive fine oak table surrounded by oversized leather chairs. The room was more appropriate for a company board meeting. I was in disbelief once I realized the RCMP planned to question me in such an ordinary environment. I had imagined they would put me in a small room with a desk and chair and very little lighting in order to put pressure on me and distort my thoughts. They kept surprising me. Or maybe I had just seen too many cop shows.

Still, I wasn't about to question why they brought me to this room instead. I sat on one side of the table, alone, looking directly across at two RCMP officers and two other people I believed to be FBI agents, one of whom was the woman from the van. There was nothing on the table except for a folder placed in front of them. The elevator ride and walk to the room had been in silence. Now we sat, still in silence. I decided to break it.

"I don't have anything to say to you, and I'm not interested in cooperating," I told them.

They seemed surprised that I would make such a definitive statement. Truth is, I had been preparing to say those words. Corporal Gosselin reached for the folder, opened it, and started to list the charges to be laid against me. He was trying to scare me.

"Well, Michael," he said, "you have a long list of charges here and not many options. You can choose to work and cooperate with us and we will work out the case against you, or you can say nothing and appear in court and take your chances."

I had already decided to hang on to my pride rather than be a stool pigeon and go against the unwritten hacker code of never divulging information to the authorities. I wanted to stand up to them. I gave him my best stare and said, "I'm not interested."

I tried to be rude about it. I didn't want to stay in that room with them, no matter how comfortable the chairs were. Corporal Gosselin began to work on me a little, asking me if I understood the seriousness of the crimes. He told me they would prosecute me relentlessly if I were to oppose them and not cooperate.

This was more along the lines of what I had expected. This was the situation I had been preparing myself for.

I realized they also wanted my help to catch other hackers. But I figured that his insistence that I cooperate meant the police were going to have a hard time proving to a judge that it was me behind the computer launching the attacks. They had my computer, but they didn't have my hard drive. So what did they have? Well, my dad for one thing. And that just started making me angry.

"I don't care how many charges you list, I'm not interested in talking or negotiating with you," I said.

That was it. Corporal Gosselin realized I was standing my ground and wasn't going to budge. He turned to the officer on his left and told him to take me for processing.

I stood up and followed the officer out the door. He led me into a room that seemed to have been prepped for my arrival. In a matter of minutes they took my fingerprints and photo, then led me back to the conference room.

I entered the room expecting to see the same four faces, but we had a visitor. It was Yan Romanowski, my lawyer and friend of the family. The only person I would have been happier to see was my father. Yan had made excellent time, and now the odds weren't so stacked against me.

Yan introduced himself for the benefit of everyone, then requested that he and I be left alone in the room for ten minutes. Once the officers had left, I told Yan what had happened up to that point. He asked how I would like to proceed, and I told him I had no desire to cooperate with the authorities. He nodded. Yan already knew that. He already knew just about everything.

After the surprises the police had sprung on my family and me that night, I finally felt as though we had the upper hand. Not only did I have a lawyer present in record time, but he knew my case and how to proceed. But only I knew my hard drive was nowhere to be found. That was my own little surprise.

"Don't worry, I will have you out Monday morning," Yan told me.

Another surprise.

It was by now early Saturday morning and I had expected to be released that day. But this was another element of the cops' plan: to arrest me on the weekend so I wouldn't be able to get a bail hearing until Monday morning. They wanted me to sit in jail over the weekend, to make things as tough on me as possible. Once I realized that, it made me more resolved not to give an inch. From the beginning, I had no desire to cooperate with the police, but now any possibility of that happening—no matter how minute—had disappeared.

Yan let the officers know we were done, and they came back into the room and sat down again. Yan asked who was in charge, and Corporal Gosselin identified himself as the head investigator on my case. He was confident.

Yan shot him a dismissive look and said, "My client has nothing to discuss. You can go ahead and book him. We will see you Monday morning."

Yan is a professional guy. He carries himself well, and he's not easily intimidated. The words he spoke to Corporal Gosselin were polite, but as far as I was concerned at the time, he was telling all the officers to go fuck themselves. Their tactics hadn't worked. That was the best I had felt since receiving the call at Patrick's house hours earlier.

I could tell the officers were pissed about the fast appearance of my lawyer and that they weren't going to have more time to talk to me alone. Good, I thought.

"Tough it out for the weekend; I'll request your bail on Monday," Yan whispered to me reassuringly. He seemed confident the judge wouldn't remand a juvenile with no prior record. Corporal Gosselin informed Yan I would be spending the weekend at a juvenile prison called Cité Des Prairies and that he and my family could visit me there. With that, it was back into another unmarked van for the drive to jail.

The encounter at the RCMP headquarters had energized me, but exhaustion took over on the ride to jail. I could hardly keep my eyes open. I didn't care what kind of place I was headed to; as long as there was a bed, it was fine with me.

CHAPTER THREE

Weekend
at Cité Des Prairies

LOOKING OUT THE VAN WINDOW, I could see we were approaching a large concrete structure surrounded by a fence topped with razor wire. The Saturday morning sun was rising, reminding me that I had been up all night. We pulled in to Cité Des Prairies, a youth detention centre. It would be my home for the weekend. The ride, and what came before it, had left me in a state of exhaustion. Everything was blurry: the building, the time of day, who I was with.

Once in the building, I was quickly searched, processed, and led to an empty cell. As soon as I hit the bed, I was out. I didn't bother with a blanket or pillow. Except for briefly opening my eyes when a guard passed by on his rounds, I didn't wake up until the other boys were already out of their cells and milling around in the common area. Because of my early-morning arrival, the guards had let me sleep in.

I rose from the bed and looked out at the scene in front of me. *So this is jail.* In less than twelve hours, I had gone from a typical Friday night sleepover at a friend's house to waking up in a facility for young offenders. I wiped the sleep from my eyes as reality set in.

I was let out to join the others and soon spotted a familiar face. His name was Quincy and he was a bit of a badass at

25

school. It wasn't a shock to see him there. He was also a big guy, the kind you'd want to have on your side in jail. I felt more sure of myself when I saw him and he greeted me. He was surprised to find me there.

Quincy showed me the ropes, which weren't too difficult to grasp considering that weekends at Cité Des Prairies consisted mostly of sitting around and playing cards or board games. When he asked me why I was there, I told him it was for breaking and entering. I didn't want to bother trying to explain my crimes. I passed the weekend playing cards with him and others. I felt protected. I could handle this.

During my time there, I thought constantly about my arrest, the raid at my house, and my dad, who I believed was also spending the weekend in jail. I kept it all inside, not wanting to draw attention to myself. My father's arrest gnawed at me all weekend. I hated that he was also in jail; I knew it was because of me. Yet I had no idea why the police had arrested him, or how they came to do so.

I would later discover that, unbeknownst to us, the police had installed a wiretap at our house to listen in on conversations and track online activity. They recorded my father raging over a business deal that had gone bad. A guy had screwed him over and my father said nasty things while on the phone with a friend. The police in turn used that to arrest him on the night of the raid for conspiracy to commit aggravated assault. When he went in front of a judge, my father agreed to stay away from the man, and that was that. They had nothing because my father had no intention of harming anyone. He was pissed off about business and let off some steam over the phone. For that, the police had arrested him. Their pressure tactics made him only more resolved to see me stand up for myself.

Although jail wasn't where I wanted to be, at least I had a friend there. Still, I couldn't wait to go before the judge on Monday. I wanted out of Cité Des Prairies.

I WAS AWOKEN EARLY ON MONDAY, APRIL 17, and told to get ready to head to the courthouse, where I was placed in a large room that looked like it had once been a cafeteria. A guard sat at a desk near the entrance. Tables and chairs were set up, and a buffet of reheated food stood congealing at one end. I could hear noise coming from a smaller room off to the side. There I discovered a group of kids playing *Mike Tyson's Punch-Out!!* on Nintendo. I waited my turn, then proceeded to run the table with them, knocking everybody out one after another. Playing video games was a normal activity for me; I felt one step closer to getting back to life as I knew it.

I was soon called to the main desk, but I wasn't sure if it was for my bail hearing or another surprise cooked up by the police. A guard led me into a small meeting room down the hall. I was relieved to find my father and Yan sitting on the other side of the glass divide. My stepmother had visited over the weekend and told me that my father had been released from jail, which was a huge relief for me. Now it was my turn to be released.

Yan and my dad began by asking if I was okay. Had anything happened in jail? Had anyone touched or bothered me? I told them I was okay and that nothing untoward had happened.

My father told me that my grandfather had offered to bring in his lawyer to take on my case. I could choose to keep Yan as my counsel or opt to go with the new lawyer. "It's up to you," my dad said. "Yan is who I recommend, and I feel confident with him if you do as well."

I didn't have to think about it. Yan had already shown his commitment by getting up in the middle of the night and rushing down to meet me at RCMP headquarters. He seemed in total control every second we were together. I had complete confidence in him.

"I want to use Yan," I said.

Yan told me I would have my bail hearing soon. He said I would be released that day, albeit with certain conditions. I couldn't wait for my hearing. I wanted to go home.

After the meeting, I was escorted back into the holding area. It wasn't long before my name was called again. This time I walked into another meeting room and found my mother and stepfather. A man I didn't know was sitting with them. It was the first time my mother had seen me since my arrest. Again, they all wanted to know what had happened to me in jail. The man with them turned out to be a lawyer. My mother and stepfather said they would pay for my defence and handle everything if I chose to use their lawyer. It was reassuring to know that my entire family was looking out for me.

I was already committed to Yan, but even if I'd had doubts about him, I wouldn't have chosen my mother and stepfather's lawyer. I liked the way Yan presented and handled himself. Something about this lawyer was off-putting. He hadn't said much, but it was enough for me to know that Yan would be my lawyer. End of discussion. I soon headed back to the holding area and waited for my bail hearing, half wondering if another relative would show up with yet another lawyer.

Finally, my name was called. Two guards took me on the elevator down to the courtroom, which we entered through the back door. The seats in the courtroom were packed. I began to worry that everyone was there to see me. As far as I knew, the police hadn't made any public announcement, but it seemed to me that too many people were there to watch the proceedings, including men in overcoats who looked like they were with the government or law enforcement. Were the other people with the press? This wasn't good. I looked around suspiciously, wondering what it all meant.

I was being paranoid. There was no press; the people there weren't any more interested in my case than anyone else's that day. But that would soon change.

After a short wait, my case was called. I was charged with two counts of criminal mischief for an online attack against CNN.com on February 8 that had caused the site to experience serious problems serving content to visitors. I faced a maximum of two years of detention and a possible fine of up to $1000. Considering I had attacked several websites, it was a relief to be charged with only two counts. I had expected more. I stood next to Yan as he entered a plea of not guilty.

The judge accepted the plea and set out a series of bail conditions. I was not allowed to use the internet or any computers, except under adult supervision. I had to stay away from places like libraries, which had free access to computers, and I wasn't to use a cellphone with internet access. I also wasn't allowed to see three of my best friends, and a curfew was imposed on me.

I understood why some of the conditions were necessary, but my school friends had nothing to do with the attacks. As for the curfew, I was usually at home all night anyway. In fact, that was where I'd launched the attacks from. I thought things seemed somewhat blown out of proportion. First with the media reports about the attacks, and then with the way the RCMP had arrested my father and me. Now I was forbidden from seeing certain friends. What did they have to do with the case? It seemed like an extra bit of punishment tacked on for good measure. That pissed me off. Even though I knew I was guilty, I was beginning to feel hard done by.

I see now that the authorities were cautious and uncertain; they'd never dealt with a case like mine before. One technology

analyst firm estimated the damage from the attacks I had orchestrated at close to US$2 billion. A fifteen-year-old kid using a
home computer had apparently caused close to a couple of
billion dollars' worth of damage. Everybody was freaking out.
They didn't know how to deal with the larger issues of online
security. The next best thing was to make an example of me in
order to put the public at ease. It seemed to be less about me and
more about what I represented: the potential for the growing
online world to be destroyed, or at least crippled, by nefarious
hackers. I needed to be held up as an example of what happens
to people who mess with the internet and e-commerce.

Anxious to get home, I agreed to the conditions and was led
back to the holding area, where I signed a document setting out
my bail conditions. Then, just like in the movies, I was handed a
brown envelope filled with my possessions and released. I thanked
my mother for coming to see me, then headed out with Yan
and my father for a strategy session. We went to Elio Pizzeria so
I could eat some good food while we planned for the coming
onslaught. I hadn't eaten much while in custody, and despite the
nature of our conversation, that meal remains one of the best
meals of my life.

Yan had requested that all evidence the police had relating to
my case be handed over to us. We would soon see exactly what
they had on me. For now, though, I just wanted some pizza and
my own bed. These larger issues could wait until the case moved
forward, which I thought would take weeks or even months.

I was wrong. The FBI, RCMP, and U.S. Attorney General had
other plans for me. At the same time as my father, Yan, and I were
conferring in Montreal, law enforcement agencies were planning
their next move. In Washington, D.C., the Attorney General was
preparing her department's response to the attacks and my arrest.
The RCMP were also prepping for their press conference.

Because I had been arrested in Canada, they would have the pleasure of being the first to announce the news that Mafiaboy had been caught. The RCMP, U.S. Attorney General, and FBI would take their time to prepare their announcements and reveal my arrest two days later, on Wednesday, April 19. Then all hell would break loose.

I enjoyed my pizza, then went home to sleep in my own bed. At that point, I had been charged with only two counts of criminal mischief. That was enough to get me offline. But the authorities' main case was yet to come.

The cops preened for their big moment. The elusive, dangerous hacker had been caught. And now they could reveal their trophy—a fifteen-year-old kid.

CHAPTER FOUR

Media Circus

AT 10:30 A.M. ON WEDNESDAY, APRIL 19, the RCMP held a press conference in Montreal. As the officers delivered the news to the assembled press, I was in class, unaware that my arrest was being announced to the world.

Inspector Yves Roussel told reporters that when it came to my crimes, "we're talking about a thousand sites across the world." That was a borderline inaccurate statement. I had been charged with two counts related to an attack on CNN.com, and now the inspector was declaring that I had attacked "about a thousand" websites. He was likely referring to the fact that, at the time, CNN.com also hosted a large number of other websites. Although I was certainly guilty of more than just the attack on CNN, the inspector had inflated the number.

An FBI spokesperson in Montreal said my arrest was "especially important to the FBI and to law enforcement around the world." This was because "unlike most crimes, cyber criminals know no boundaries and respect no sovereignty. Theirs is a world contained only by the breadth of the internet."

Even before the press conference started, major television networks and newswires were reporting my arrest. The evening before, ABC broke the news that the RCMP had arrested someone in connection with the Mafiaboy case. Early on

Wednesday morning, NBC's *Today Show*, CNN, and others were already reporting that a teenager had been arrested in Montreal. "A fifteen-year-old boy has been arrested in connection with those very serious cyber attacks that took place earlier this year," said one CNN anchor before the press conference began. After the RCMP released more details, the newswires and networks continued to treat my arrest as a major story. Then, a few minutes past noon, U.S. Attorney General Janet Reno spoke with reporters on Capitol Hill.

"I think that it's important first of all that we look at what we've seen and let young people know that they are not going to be able to get away with something like this scot-free," she said. "There has got to be a remedy, there has got to be a penalty. I believe this recent breakthrough demonstrates our capacity to track down those who would abuse this remarkable new technology, and track them down wherever they may be."

I had returned to school the day before and acted as though nothing had happened. No one knew that I had been arrested early Saturday morning or that I was in court on Monday. Except for the one friend I had told, no one at school knew I was Mafiaboy. Tuesday passed like any other school day. Wednesday, however, would be unlike any other day in my life.

After the RCMP press conference finished, reporters piled into their vehicles and sped to my high school. Although Canadian law forbade the police from releasing my name because I was a young offender, they did say that I was a student at Riverdale High School. So every major media outlet with staff in Montreal rushed to the school. By the time lunch was finished, there was a sea of news trucks and reporters in front of the building. They yelled questions at passing students ("Do you know who Mafiaboy is?") and did their best to get as many people on camera as possible. I hadn't been aware of the press conference, and so the resulting media circus at my school left me shaken.

I had worked for years to keep my online activities separate from the rest of my life. Suddenly, reporters and cameras were at my school. They knew Mafiaboy went there, and it was only a matter of time before they learned who I was, what I looked like—if they didn't already. I couldn't hide behind a handle anymore. This was one of the moments when I realized how out of control the situation was going to get. I had already seen my hacker name broadcast on CNN and other networks. The RCMP, FBI, and other law enforcement agencies had raided my home and arrested my father and me. But looking out at the crush of reporters, I realized things were likely going to keep getting stranger, and more difficult. This was bigger than I had ever imagined.

I stayed inside the school, not knowing if the reporters knew my name or what I looked like. I was hanging out with Vito, one of my school friends, and talking about the scene outside when I decided to let him in on my secret. I told him the press was there for me, that I was Mafiaboy. It took me a few minutes to convince him. Then Vito hatched a plan to get the heat off me.

I watched Vito walk out of the school and swagger up to the gaggle of cameras and reporters. He told the assembled press that he knew Mafiaboy's real name and then proceeded to reveal it. Except Vito didn't offer me up—he picked another student at the school, somebody we thought was kind of a loser. He told the press that that student was their man. It was as though he had thrown raw meat into a tiger cage. I could see the reporters taking great pains to spell the name correctly as they wrote in their notebooks. Then the questions continued for Vito and everyone else. They interrogated every student they could in

order to gather as much information as possible about the student
Vito had named. There was such mayhem that the boy was sent
home from school early. I heard that the press followed him to
his house.

As much as the situation was freaking me out, Vito managed to
give me a laugh and help me feel a little bit better. I was so
concerned about my own circumstances that I didn't feel any
remorse over what we had done to that student. I regret the trouble
I must have caused him. I can only imagine how frightened and
confused he and his family must have been.

By that time, the police had notified the school that I was the
culprit. Soon the vice-principal, whom I never got along with,
was out dealing with the press and explaining that they had been
given the wrong name. Even though he didn't reveal my name,
the vice-principal had no qualms about telling the press that
Mafiaboy was a troubled student. He acted as if he wasn't
surprised I was Mafiaboy. The press soon figured out my name,
as did my fellow students, though I still don't know how. The
school called my father and said it was best for me to head home
because the media frenzy was disturbing everyone at the school.

I knew the press would likely be camped out at our house,
so I took a route home through a golf course that bordered my
backyard. I managed to sneak in unseen, having avoided the
front entrance. Once inside, I peeked out a window and saw
that the street was lined with media trucks. All the major
Canadian news outlets were there, satellite dishes and antennas
pointing skyward, ready to beam out any new information
gleaned about me. I hid inside the house and tried to grapple
with the reality that, after being hunted by the FBI and RCMP,
I was now being chased by the media. It wasn't going to stop.
The phone was ringing constantly and some reporters even
tried the doorbell.

Late in the afternoon, I saw my brother, Lorenzo, coming up the street. As soon as they saw him, the reporters descended on him, firing off questions and jostling for the best shot. Lorenzo walked past them as quickly as he could. He had a big grin on his face as he walked in the front door, but he was also pissed off. "Bro, what the fuck is going on?" he yelled.

I felt bad for Lorenzo. Only a few nights before, he had come home to find our street filled with cars and our house being torn apart by police officers. Now he was returning from what had been just a regular day at his school to see the street lined with media trucks and to have a group of reporters shoving microphones in his face. It could have been a scene in a movie. He was laughing because of the absurdity of it all; he couldn't believe what was happening. We marvelled at the scene outside.

"Don't fucking go out there," he told me.

I had no desire to. I wondered what the neighbours were thinking, and what was being said and written about me and my family. I could see reporters talking with neighbours, some of whom, as it turned out, said nice things about me. Others took the opportunity to slam me and my father. One reporter would later write that neighbours described my father as a "husky, brash, unrefined loudmouth who liked to sit in front of his house in a sweatsuit yelling and cursing into a cell phone."

My father arrived home a few hours later. He pulled into the driveway in his Range Rover and got out, a cigar in his mouth. The press ran toward him, but he waved them off and repeated "No comment" until he got through the front door.

Reporters continued to call the house and ring the doorbell. Some walked to the side of the house, trying to get a glimpse inside a window. Before long, my school called and my father agreed it would be best for me to stay home for the rest of the week.

The trucks and reporters remained outside our house for the next three or four days. Meanwhile, I was trapped inside.

FOR THE NEXT COUPLE OF DAYS, I sat next to my brother as he went online and read aloud the articles about me. My bail conditions forbade me from using a home computer, so Lorenzo became my proxy on the internet. We needed only to pick a media website at random and inevitably there would be a story about me on it. The story was building to such a frenzy that Yan decided to speak with a reporter from *The New York Times* to set a few things straight. On Saturday, April 22, the paper published an article about me and my family.

"It is the picture of North American suburban normalcy: a new four-bedroom house on the edge of a golf course, an orange basketball left outside in the rain by the 15-year-old son, a soggy cigar butt left outside on a plastic chair by Dad," it began. "But according to the Canadian and American police, the 15-year-old basketball player is Mafiaboy, for the moment North America's most notorious computer crime suspect."

Speaking to *The New York Times* about my criminal history before this incident, Yan said, "He has never committed nor been accused of any criminal offence nor has he been involved with police authorities." He also expressed what we at home were thinking: "We hope that this media thing dies down fast, so he can get back to a normal life, so that it doesn't jeopardize his school year."

The previous day, *The Washington Post* had published a lengthy story that toed the police line, suggesting that my father had hired a hit man to hurt his former associate, which, of course, was false. The story also focused on my problems at school. That part was true. "Known as a computer whiz but a constant discipline problem—he had been suspended from Riverdale twice this year—he frequently talked back to his English and math teachers, banging his desk and rarely showing up for class with books and completed homework," was how the newspaper summarized comments from people at school. According to the story, I also "hung out generally with the tough guys and was known to smoke cigarettes."

Not exactly a flattering portrait. I was "North America's most notorious computer crime suspect," a backtalking, cigarette-smoking little punk. Other reports emphasized my penchant for baggy clothes and wearing baseball caps backward. Everyone seemed in agreement—Mafiaboy was a perfect hoodlum. It made for great copy. Aside from his conversation with *The New York Times,* Yan was more focused on the case than controlling the media. This meant anybody who claimed to know me was handed a megaphone to say whatever he or she wanted.

I admit a part of me was flattered to hear law enforcement initially speak about me in lofty terms. At the press conference on Wednesday, I was made to sound like some kind of evil genius. But the authorities also exaggerated the facts and realities of the case, and this wasn't good for me and my situation. Worse, the press seemed happy to play along.

"The arrest represents a stunning potential breakthrough for authorities in one of the most high-profile hacking sprees in history and a crime that many security experts believed might never be solved," reported the *Los Angeles Times* on its website the day my arrest was announced.

The paper also noted that "much of the Internet community still is recovering from February's attacks, which caused millions of dollars in disruptions and damage, affected millions of Internet users and prompted such alarm among security experts that President Clinton held a White House summit on the issue and pressed for greater funding to fight 'cyber crime.' "

Already, the estimate of damage from the attacks had shrunk from close to $2 billion to "hundreds of millions." And yet, according to the RCMP, I was guilty of hacking something around a thousand websites. It was interesting—and extremely frustrating—to see numbers and figures and descriptions of me thrown around by law enforcement, the press, and so-called experts. I knew I had attacked several of the internet's biggest e-commerce sites and had compromised hundreds of servers to get the job done, but I couldn't see how this translated into hundreds of millions of dollars in damage. My attacks shut the sites down; I hadn't stolen credit card numbers or ruined any equipment. At the time, I was angry that no one seemed to be telling the truth about my crimes.

Along with the hard facts offered about my arrest, there was a huge amount of inaccuracy. One newspaper reported that I lived close to RCMP headquarters in Westmount. Even before my arrest, some reports had placed Mafiaboy in Toronto. Incorrect. Law enforcement and the press were painting a detailed portrait of me and my crimes, yet I hadn't sat down and spoken with any of them. The people telling my story in and outside the press didn't know the truth, and they certainly didn't know me.

I did what Yan told me and kept my mouth shut. And so the conflicting tales of the mysterious teenage hacker named Mafiaboy continued to dominate the news. I was being turned into a media myth. Somebody eventually registered the domain mafiaboy.com and began advocating on my behalf. He also started selling merchandise. Hacker sites criticized the police and press for their scare tactics and lack of hard information about the case. Security experts spent their days being interviewed about the case. Everybody was piling on, and I was sitting at home, silent.

One of the most fascinating things during the media frenzy was the RCMP's attempt (after celebrating the capture of the person who had attacked "about a thousand" websites) to control the public's perception of me and what I had done. In a *New York Times* article published April 20, RCMP inspector Yves Roussel is quoted as saying, "Mafiaboy wasn't the best. He was not what we would call a genius in that field."

A few days earlier, I was a potential menace to society who warranted an early-morning raid, the arrest of my father on bogus charges, and a press conference on Capitol Hill held by the U.S. Attorney General. Now, I was just some dumb kid. The police had been happy to crow about my capture as if it were a major strike against cybercrime, but now they didn't want anyone to get the impression that I was anything special. Maybe they didn't want me to become a celebrity like Kevin Mitnick, an infamous hacker who was the target of a major manhunt by the FBI, the inspiration for films, and the subject of a book by *New York Times* reporter John Markoff. Mitnick's time on the lam from the FBI turned him into a celebrity hacker, the kind who inspires others to imitate him. The kind of hacker people root for as he evades police and government agents.

Mitnick also saw his reputation and crimes manipulated by the press and law enforcement. "I got into trouble largely because of my actions," he admitted to CNN in a 2005 interview. "However, because of the media reporting, I was treated as 'Osama bin Mitnick.'"

I was in this situation because of what I'd done, but it felt like things were already completely out of control. No one seemed to appreciate the conflicted messages coming out of the mouths of law-enforcement officials. One day I was a brazen hacker bringing e-commerce to its knees; the next I was just a silly little "script kiddie," a wannabe hacker with little or no skill. The press ate it up.

So was I really some kind of wunderkind hacker, or just a young punk piggybacking on the work of others?

As is usually the case, the truth was somewhere in between.

CHAPTER FIVE

Portrait of the Hacker as a Young Man

THE MODERN HISTORY OF MY FAMILY begins in 1954 when a strapping teenager stepped off a ship and onto Canadian soil for the first time. Up until that point, Lorenzo Calce had lived his life in Italy. He spoke no English but was determined to make a new life in his adopted country. He had less than $100 in his pocket.

Lorenzo soon landed a job in Montreal washing taxis and later worked shining shoes at the tony Queen Elizabeth Hotel. That's what he was doing at age nineteen when Charles Hershorn, the owner of Limousine Murray Hill, began stopping to have his shoes shined. Hershorn took note of the young man's enthusiasm for the work, the way he buffed shoes to a gleaming polish.

"I could use a young man like you," Hershorn told him.

Lorenzo began shining Hershorn's fleet of limousines. After just three months, he was moved to the body shop to learn how to fix the company's vehicles. He soon became a master mechanic, specializing in buses. Then he was promoted to manager of the entire garage.

Just two years after arriving in Canada, Lorenzo created a new design for a sightseeing bus and would go on to design and manufacture many more. By 1966, at the age of thirty-one, he was vice-president of the company; by 1982 he owned his own bus company, Autocar Connaisseur Inc., which would grow to earn annual revenues of more than $20 million.

Lorenzo is my grandfather. He's the patriarch of the family, the namesake of my older brother, and the kind of immigrant success story that everyone loves to hear. In our family, he's *the* final word. Unless, of course, my grandmother, Immacolata, has something to say.

Like my grandfather, my father has spent much of his life working with buses. He quit his job at a bank to help my grandfather launch and run Connaisseur. They sold the company in 1997, and my father works at another bus company to this day.

Because of the hard work of my grandfather and father, my family lived well. Growing up, we had a large house, and my brother and I had all the things any kids could want or need. Plus, when my school basketball team needed to travel to an away game, there was always a big, comfortable bus ready to take us to our destination. You might call me spoiled, except our house had rules.

My mother and father each had their own way of parenting. My mom was stricter and laid down the rules by assigning weekly chores, checking to see that my homework was done, and handing out discipline. She also increased my intelligence more than any institution or school by constantly pushing me to learn and expand my horizons. She was always giving me books to read and Mensa problems to complete. I liked solving problems, figuring things out. And I liked doing so on my own.

My dad, on the other hand, was a successful entrepreneur who taught me about business and how to make a living. He also taught me what hackers refer to as social-engineering skills. Most folks know them as people skills—how to talk to someone, how to negotiate, and how to size someone up. My father knew everybody. He had the gift of interacting easily with people. He believed in setting rules and discipline, but he had a freer attitude than my mom. This was a source of friction between them.

I never set out to break the rules as a kid. But some rules are meant to be broken; living life in a straight line according to the rules of others is not always the best path. People have to challenge conventions and question the status quo. That doesn't necessarily mean breaking the law, but I believe it's important to be true to yourself. Like any kid, I didn't always follow the rules set out for me at home or at school. Still, the combination of my parents' methods of parenting gave me many benefits, even if I didn't always take advantage of them. But for most of my life, they haven't been together in the same house, or in marriage.

I was five years old when my parents separated. It wasn't easy to see them battle for custody. It was an ugly dispute that lingers to this day. My brother, Lorenzo, and I were the prizes they were fighting for, but we didn't feel lucky at the time. After a long battle, my mother won primary custody over my brother and me; my father had us every second weekend. I can tell you first-hand, as can any young child who watched their parents separate, that divorce can shred a kid's life. There was constant tension between my mom and dad, and I was suddenly splitting my life between two parents, two homes. It's not in my personality to sulk about things, and so at the time I focused on keeping myself distracted with friends and activities. It was easy to occupy myself at my mom's house because my friends were in the neighbourhood. We would play on the swing set in the backyard or play Nintendo games in the basement.

My father moved out of the family home and into a condo downtown. I didn't know anyone in the area, and there wasn't much to do when I stayed with him. My dad was, and is, a total workaholic. He loved spending time with me on the weekends, but work would inevitably come calling. He had a business to run. A bus would break down, or a driver would call in sick. It was an unpredictable business, and he was the one people called when things went bad.

My first weekend at his new place was boring and unremarkable. I spent most of the time watching TV and sitting around. After seeing how bored I was, my dad decided to get me something to occupy my time and challenge me. I was six years old and loved playing video games. Systems such as Nintendo had become hugely popular and the video game industry was growing and advancing. So too were personal computers, though I hadn't used one. As for the internet, it was still relatively unknown in 1991. The World Wide Web hadn't gone public yet. Those people who were online were mainly academics, government employees, the military, and computer geeks. At age six, I was none of these things. Not yet, at least.

When I arrived at my dad's condo the next Friday night, he told me he had a present for me. I had no idea what it could be, but it turned out to be a gift that would forever change my life. It was, of course, a computer.

Its configuration is still burned into my memory: an Intel 486 running Windows 3.11 with DOS 4.0. It was a standard computer for the time, but it was thousands of times slower than the average PC in today's homes. The smartphones people carry around with them today are more powerful than that old box was. To me, though, it was an amazing machine, even if I knew next to nothing about it or how it worked. My first impulse was to use it to play games. The original *Mario Bros.* game on Nintendo and other titles like *Zelda* had already captivated me. I wondered what a machine like this could do. It was, after all, a real computer and not a toy for kids.

My other hobbies at the time were playing with LEGO and collecting hockey cards. Because of my father's bus company,

I had a nice collection of cards signed by NHL players. Whenever the Quebec NHL teams needed to travel by bus, they called his company. I remember my father taking me to the dressing room at one game and coming face to face with a naked Joe Sakic, one of my heroes who at that time was a star for the Quebec Nordiques. He signed my card, as did many of the other players, including Wayne Gretzky. I treasured those cards.

But the computer was something entirely new. It had come from my dad's office, so there were no games to be found on its hard drive. I nagged him to buy me a game to load onto the computer, but I also started exploring the machine to see what it could do. Over the first few weekends, I quickly went from not knowing how to do anything to using DOS commands to make the computer perform certain operations. I devoured the manuals my father brought for me, trying everything they suggested and using that knowledge to experiment. It was like receiving a new set of LEGO. First I would build what the directions dictated, then I used those same pieces to create something entirely new.

Soon, the delay between sessions with the computer began to drive me crazy. It's hard for me to explain even to this day why that computer had such an instant hold on me. I can remember sitting and listening to it beep, gurgle, and churn as it processed commands. I remember how the screen lit up in front of my face. Unlike a TV or video game system, I could dictate what the computer did, down to the smallest of functions. The screen beckoned me to give it commands; the noises told me it was doing my bidding. The computer gave me, a six year old, a sense of control, of limitless possibility. My life was filled with so many things I couldn't control: school, family, adults, rules, chores. A computer didn't know I was just a kid. As long as I gave it the right command, it would do whatever I wanted. Nothing else in my world operated that way.

I was fascinated and wanted to play on it non-stop, but I had access to it only every other weekend. In the interim, I thought about the next experiment to try with my new toy. I quickly went from dragging my feet to prepare for the trip to my dad's to getting my stuff ready and waiting at the front door for him to pick me up. I was hooked. I was also happy and occupied, and that made my dad feel good about taking me away from my friends on weekends.

My father didn't question my computer usage. It was the weekend and his condo was in downtown Montreal. I was too young to go anywhere on my own and too far away from friends to hang out with them. We didn't have internet access, so everything I did on my 486 was self-contained, so to speak. It was just me and my box. I instantly thought of it as *mine*. I put in the time to learn how it worked and was rewarded with more knowledge. Gradually, I went from playing games such as *King's Quest* to learning how to use diagnostic tools and update drivers. My computer knowledge was increasing, and I had a hunger to learn more. That meant I needed to spend every second possible on the computer.

Years passed, with me playing games on and learning via the computer. In the meantime, I went to school, hung out with friends, and played sports. The reality of my parents' divorce set in, and eventually our family grew because of it. Within a few years of their divorce, both my mother and father remarried, and my brother and I soon found ourselves with a half-sister and new step-siblings.

My mother married a man named Robert. Their house was refined and disciplined. Before long, my mom gave birth to a baby girl, Natasha, my half-sister. My father married Carole, who had two kids of her own, a boy and girl. Derek is a year older than I am, and Jen is the same age as Lorenzo, who is three years older than I am. I would see them when I visited my dad on weekends and on holidays, and I liked being in a house where there were always people around. It also made it easy for me to sneak off and spend hours on the computer. And whenever I had the chance, that's exactly what I did.

I CAN STILL SEE THE PACKAGE. It was a flat, square envelope with a CD inside. The message printed on the front made it clear it had something to do with computers. It was 1993, I was nine years old, and my perspective on computers was about to undergo a major shift.

The package, which sat on top of a pile of mail at my dad's house, was from a company called America Online—AOL. I'd never heard of it. It promised free access to the internet—games! chat!—for thirty days. All I needed was a modem.

I had to ask myself, what's a modem and where do I get one? These were new terms to me: internet, online, modem. The concepts were fuzzy, yet exciting. I could download and play games online with other people? I could converse with someone thousands of miles away? I wanted in. I wanted a modem. And, like any nine year old who wants something, there was only one way to get it. I started begging my father.

"You want a fax machine?"

That was my dad's response when I asked him to buy me a modem. He didn't know what one was. But things were still tense between him and my mom, and if getting me a modem would make me happy, he didn't see why not. As far as he was concerned, if it had to do with computers, it was educational. I got my modem, installed it, and immediately loaded the AOL CD. Suddenly, it was no longer about only me and my box. I had a sense that there were others like me out there. I wanted to find them. AOL appeared to offer that opportunity.

AOL made its name, and a lot of money, by making the internet easy and friendly for millions of people, even if its target demographic wasn't exactly nine-year-old kids. Within a few minutes of registering for my free thirty days of access, I was online. Staring at the computer screen, I was bursting with excitement. There was a whole world out there for me to discover! And yet I just kept staring, because I had no idea how to start. What should I search for?

My first thought was games. I started looking for games I could play online or download. Then I tested out AOL's chat function. I began flowing in and out of chat rooms dedicated to different topics. The most popular by far were the dating chat rooms. Men looking for women, women looking for men, men looking for men ... everybody seemed to be there, looking for somebody, flirting with one another. It struck me as pretty ridiculous.

I wanted games to download onto my computer and play on my own time. I had heard you could download versions of even the most popular games for free. This was a type of "warez"— pirated software. I started looking for warez chat channels and managed to find some. From that point on, I would go online and hunt for games I could download. I didn't care about much else until one day I was in a chat room hanging out and asking about warez. I usually pretended to be someone other than me—an adult—and guessed I was being annoying because the next thing I knew, I was kicked out of the chat room and my AOL connection was lost. *What the hell was that?*

I logged back on and began paying closer attention. I realized it was a common occurrence and that it was called punting. Someone knocked me offline by hitting me with so much data that my connection was severed. These punters seemed to have a huge amount of power over others on AOL. I was intrigued that an individual was able to "attack" someone else, regardless of the distance between them, using the internet. It seemed like harmless fun, almost a practical joke. The people punted off could simply sign on again and rejoin the chat room. Nobody got hurt.

I wanted to punt someone. Badly.

I started browsing the net for applications that would help me punt, and maybe more. It took some time for me to figure out how to find them, my free internet running out all the while. I wasn't sure if my dad would give me his credit card number to purchase the service—especially because of what had happened with the LEGO. Some time earlier, my father had made the mistake of leaving me with his credit card. Thrilled with my new-found purchasing power, I called in an order of LEGO. Soon after, a stack of boxes arrived at our house. I had pretty much picked my way through the LEGO catalogue, and now our garage seemed filled with it. I hadn't seen the card since.

Realizing that I might lose the battle for his card, I rushed to gather every application and game I could get my hands on. One application I found enabled me to enter a chat room disguised as an AOL staff member. AOL staff often entered chats to warn users about inappropriate behaviour or other violations of the terms of service. (They were highlighted onscreen in a special way so other users could see their status.)

Users trusted the staff designation and so, this program explained, you could use this status to "phish" for account information from other users. Basically, you fooled them into handing over information such as their login name and password. It was a scam whereby you told a user that a power outage at an AOL facility required you to ask him or her for account information. It seemed like a laughably simple trick. I tried it a few times and, to my surprise, found success on just my fourth attempt. I was amazed when I logged on with the person's user account and the password actually worked. I realized how gullible users were, so I decided to get a few more accounts just in case one closed on me. Suddenly, it didn't seem to matter whether my dad was willing to buy an account. I had taken care of it on my own.

The ease of use that enabled me, a nine year old, to get online meant that a lot of other folks with little or no knowledge of computers or the internet were also signing on to AOL. In poker, a game I love, somebody with a decent amount of money who always loses is called a fish. In the hacker community, trolling around trying to fish out sensitive information from other users is called phishing. I saw that AOL was filled with a ton of fish, so I went phishing.

That's when my real hunt for AOL hacking tools started. Once I found that first application, I stumbled across more and more. They were each brilliant in their own subversive way. I came across one site that had a huge list of applications. I decided to download all of them and browse their various functions. With these tools in hand, I began to feel like I was in control of the internet, rather than the other way around. The sense of power and possibility was intoxicating.

One of the best tools available was called AOHell. It was an all-in-one AOL shit disturber application. You could create fake accounts to pester other users from, or fashion an "email bomb" that would generate a couple of thousand email messages and send them to an unfortunate user. Because users had dial-up connections, it could take them hours to download all that mail. (I didn't "bomb" very much because it took about twenty minutes to generate the messages and launch the attack. I didn't have the attention span for that—I was only a nine-year-old kid.) AOHell could also help you phish out people's passwords and get into paid areas of AOL for free. It was a one-stop shop for messing with AOL and its customers.

"If you're an anarchist, or just hate AOL and want to fuck them over, or if you just want to use the handy utilities mentioned above this is the tool for you!" read the documentation for AOHell 3.0. "Rage Against the Machine ..."

I wasn't exactly filled with rage. For me, it was more about testing the limits and causing enough trouble to leave me laughing to myself at my keyboard. As far as I was concerned, I was lobbing data spitballs at a virtual blackboard. I gave no thought to laws; it didn't occur to me that I was breaking any.

Another tool I used was an ASCII spammer. ASCII is a standard for printable characters (basic numbers and letters) used on computers. ASCII spam was a method of using letters and numbers to flood a chat room so that no one could chat. The program also enabled users to generate images using ASCII characters: I would enter a chat room and suddenly people would see a giant middle finger where their chats used to be. It was silly and juvenile, but I got a kick out of it.

Overall, though, punting was my method of choice. I loved punting people who got on my nerves. The idea of using a flood of data to knock people offline was strangely appealing to me. My early fascination with punting would come into play again years later when I began working with a fellow hacker to build a weapon that I hoped would send rival groups fleeing for their online lives. But at this point, I was nothing more than a "kiddie." That's a term used to describe wannabe hackers who use other people's applications to wreak havoc. Kiddies, also called newbies or noobs, aren't hackers because they don't know how to write code. They often know very little about computers in general.

My knowledge of how my own PC worked was pretty high, especially for a nine year old, but I didn't know how to write software. I was learning more and more about the internet and networks, yet my overall skills were rudimentary. I was using other people's programs to stir things up online.

At that time, I didn't know what a hacker was, let alone understand that I was a kiddie, the lowest of the low. But by using other people's applications, I slowly learned how things worked. I eventually began to modify the applications to meet my needs. This is how kiddies become hackers. Everybody has to start somewhere. You can't just know everything right away.

The more I used the tools and learned how they worked, the more I became fixated with the people creating them. There were lots of kiddies on AOL doing the same things as I was, but I didn't have any interaction with the people who actually wrote the programs. They seemed like the best players in a computer game, the people who know all the tricks and secrets. The ones who control everyone else. After spending years trying to learn everything about how my PC worked, and enjoying every second of learning DOS commands and other technical information, I felt a strange kinship with these nameless, faceless programmers and online rebels. How did they create these programs? How many more of them were out there? How could I learn to write programs? To me, they were the coolest kids in cyberspace. I wanted to hang with them.

I wanted to be a hacker.

CHAPTER SIX

A Brief History
of Hacking

IN THE LATE 1950S, students walking inside Building 20 on the campus of the Massachusetts Institute of Technology were often surprised to discover a room that housed a massive model train layout. Built and maintained by the student members of the Tech Model Railroad Club, the TMRC, it was a miniature world unto itself. The layout dominated the room and came complete with "a little town, a little industrial area, a tiny working trolley line, a papier-mâché mountain, and of course a lot of trains and tracks," according to Steven Levy in his 1984 book *Hackers*.

While the trains and their surroundings were undeniably impressive, the true source of genius was a section that most people never saw. Underneath the train layout was a maze of wires and switches that made the trains run on schedule. Maintained by the club's Signals and Power Subcommittee, it was on this maze that amateur engineers spent countless hours tinkering to perfect the system, which had been donated by a phone company. The basic system had grown exponentially thanks to clever members who liberated switches, relays, and other parts from phone systems.

The members of TMRC took their toy trains seriously. They also developed their own language for talking about them.

Equipment was "losing" when not working properly. If it was completely useless, it was "munged." Garbage was "cruft." And anyone who spent his or her time doing coursework was a "tool." One term in particular became well known: *hack*. This, according to Levy, referred to a "project undertaken or a product built not solely to fulfill some constructive goal, but with some wild pleasure taken in mere involvement."

For many years on the MIT campus, a "hack" had meant a prank. But it took on new meaning in Building 20. To achieve a hack was to have done something clever and innovative with the tools at hand. The best of the Signals and Power crew were known and respected for their many hacks. They earned special status within the group—the right to call themselves hackers.

The term made the leap to the world of computing thanks in part to proximity. On the first floor of MIT Building 26 was a room that would become familiar to the hackers of TMRC. In it sat a massive IBM 704 computer, a multimillion-dollar machine with its own team of operators. They guarded the computer, maintained it, and did their best to protect it from overeager undergrads who salivated at the prospect of getting their hands on it.

Many TMRC members soon found themselves enamoured and obsessed with the giant IBM machine and the TX-0, another computer that soon found its way onto campus. That year, in 1959, MIT offered its first undergraduate course in computer programming. But many of the TMRC hackers had already begun sneaking and cajoling their way into using these new, fantastic machines. The railroaders were well beyond what was being taught in the introductory class. They had hacked their way to knowledge.

The hackers still worked on the railroad, but they also were spending their nights using the TX-0, which was easier to book time on than the IBM 704. Hacking began moving from the railway to what would eventually become the information superhighway—computers and the internet.

ALTHOUGH THE TERM *hacker* now has a negative connotation, it began as a badge of honour. In today's world some use the term *white hat hacker* to describe someone who hacks for good. A *black hat hacker*, or *cracker*, is someone who hacks with malicious intent.

Early hackers were known for attaining a high level of proficiency with computers, be it by writing programs (software) or tinkering with parts (hardware). There was no internet, no e-commerce, no email ... none of the things that brought the internet, and the concept of hackers, to the masses.

"Though some in the field used the term 'hacker' as a form of derision, implying that hackers were either nerdy social outcasts or 'unprofessional' programmers who wrote dirty, 'nonstandard' code, I found them quite different," writes Levy in *Hackers*. "Beneath their often unimposing exteriors, they were adventurers, visionaries, risk-takers, artists ... and the ones who most clearly saw why the computer was a truly revolutionary tool."

During the 1960s and 1970s, computers slowly became more mainstream, and the seeds of the internet were planted. The hackers—part engineer, part programmer, part ne'er-do-well, part entrepreneur—took the technology to new heights. The early hackers were ahead of the times. They saw that even these huge, slow, and clumsy computers had the potential to induce change on a massive scale. As computers became woven into the fabric of commerce and society, hackers created their own patterns and pulled away at loose threads left by computer manufacturers.

In the early 1960s, as the model railroad hackers continued their work at MIT, the telephone systems in the United States began using computers to switch calls. Early phone systems relied on human operators to connect calls. The new computer systems replaced them with sounds produced at set frequencies. These tonal frequencies told the central system how to direct calls. It was a sonic language largely understood only by phone company engineers, but a small group of people also learned to speak it. They were a new breed of hacker known as phone phreaks. The most famous of them was John Draper.

In 1970, a man named Denny Teresi invited Draper, an acquaintance, to witness how he and others were manipulating the phone system. In a dark room, Draper, who had served as a radar technician in the U.S. Air Force, was introduced to the world of phone phreaking. By reproducing the exact tones used to switch and connect calls within the phone system, Teresi and his fellow phreaks were able to place calls anywhere in the world. Draper was hooked.

Draper soon earned the nickname Captain Crunch because he used a toy whistle from a cereal box to help attain the frequencies necessary to make phone calls and manipulate the phone system. In the documentary film *The Secret History of Hacking,* he recalls how he and others would often walk past a bank of pay phones and blow the whistle. The people chatting away would suddenly find that their calls had been disconnected. By spending a lot of time at pay phones (the phreaks' golden rule was never to phreak from home, as the phone company could trace it), Draper, Teresi, and others eventually learned how to navigate the phone system, discovering which frequencies did what, and how to combine them. They hacked the phone system.

The phreaks also became adept at using social engineering— manipulating people into disclosing passwords or other information that will compromise a system's security—to trick phone company employees into doing their bidding. In the film, Draper describes as an example of social engineering the ability to convince a phone-company employee that you work for the company. This feat could unlock access to other parts of the system, or even the doors of the company itself. Years later, social engineering would be used by hackers such as Kevin Mitnick to gain access to company buildings, including those belonging to phone companies.

Draper became famous for using his cereal-box whistle with the blue box, a tone-generating device that could easily and reliably offer access to the phone system. With the whistle and blue box, "it was possible to take internal control of Ma Bell's long distance switching equipment," Draper writes in the essay "The Origins of Captain Crunch ..." posted on his website.

The phreaks remained a relatively small hacker community until the October 1971 issue of *Esquire* hit newsstands. The magazine contained an article titled "Secrets of the Little Blue Box." It began:

> I am in the expensively furnished living room of Al Gilbertson (his real name has been changed), the creator of the "blue box." Gilbertson is holding one of his shiny black-and-silver "blue boxes" comfortably in the palm of his hand, pointing out the thirteen little red push buttons sticking up from the console. He is dancing his fingers over the buttons, tapping out discordant beeping electronic jingles. He is trying to explain to me how his little blue box does nothing less than place the entire telephone system of the world, satellites, cables and all, at the service of the blue-box operator, free of charge.

Close to the end of the article was the story of one phreak who had been apprehended and taken to court by a phone company only to later find himself hired as a telephone-set repairman by another phone company. "It's the kind of job I dreamed about," the man was quoted as saying. "They found out about me from the publicity surrounding the trial. Maybe Ma Bell did me a favour busting me. I'll have telephones in my hands all day long."

This phreak's name was Joe Engressia. He was a blind man who realized that his perfect pitch allowed him to whistle precise tones into a phone and gain access to the system. His story was unique at the time, but decades later it would become somewhat common to see hackers hired by the businesses they had infiltrated.

The *Esquire* article set off a minor phreaking craze in the United States. Before long, possession of a blue box could get you two years in jail. Draper was at one point indicted for wire fraud and served time in jail. Captain Crunch became a cult hero to many budding hackers, two of whom decided to start creating and selling blue boxes. Their names were Steve Wozniak and Steve Jobs, and they would go on to co-found the company that today is known as Apple Inc. The pair idolized Captain Crunch and managed to persuade him to visit Wozniak's dorm room in California. Draper taught them about the blue box, and Wozniak placed a call to the Vatican. (Unfortunately, the Pope was unavailable.) Wozniak would go on to be regarded as one of the best true hackers. Jobs, of course, would become a visionary in the computer industry.

In the mid-1970s, the world's first personal computer, the Altair 8800, went on sale. It came in the form of a build-it-yourself kit and led to the creation of small computer-user clubs around the world. One was the Homebrew Computer Club in California. Jobs and Wozniak were members. The clubs became breeding grounds for hacking. Members obsessed about finding new ways to use the Altair. Many went on to hack together their own systems.

The dawn of the personal computer finally gave aspiring hackers the ability to hack away on their own system in their own homes. Members freely shared what they learned about the Altair, swapping tips about circuit boards and other technical details. They no longer had to find ways to gain access to systems owned by businesses or academic institutions, though many still did. The Homebrew hackers created a community built on an obsession with computers and the free exchange of information. This ideal became a core component of what some came to call the hacker ethic: information should be free; knowledge should be shared for the benefit of all.

Corporations and governments didn't agree. Computers were still very expensive. Their operation and the company secrets contained within them were highly confidential. These secret, powerful systems would forever remain a fixation with hackers, and many would go to jail as a result.

AS PCS SLOWLY BEGAN TRICKLING INTO HOMES, and more and more businesses began moving to computerized systems, the project that would become the internet was moving ahead. Launched in 1969, it was called ARPANET, which stood for the Advanced Research Projects Agency network. It was conceived as a way for the U.S. military to maintain command and control in the event of a nuclear attack. The idea was to build a data communications network that would allow an electronic message to be delivered even if some systems on the network had become disabled. A key innovation of ARPANET was a technology called packet switching. The data exchanged between computers were broken into small packets and sent along the wires connecting the network. With packet switching, these small bundles of data could now reach their destination by any number of available routes even if certain network nodes (computers) were unavailable. Before that advancement, the loss of one node would have brought down the entire network.

ARPANET began by connecting computers at four universities: University of California, Los Angeles (UCLA); University of

California, Santa Barbara; Stanford; and the University of Utah. A computer in Utah could now, for example, connect to the computer at UCLA and print or share files. The first email program was written in 1971 and email-driven discussion lists followed shortly after. By that year, ARPANET had grown to sixty-four nodes thanks to interest from other universities. It continued to expand and soon ARPANET joined with similar networks that had emerged. All of them began working from the same networking protocols in 1983, effectively creating the internet, a name drawn from the new, preferred protocol, transmission control protocol/internet protocol (TCP/IP). The military network that had been the original goal of ARPANET was eventually separated from the public network, the internet.

By that time, the personal computer had made huge strides. Apple Computer hit sales of US$2 billion in 1983, and the Homebrew Computer Club in California had seen twenty-three computer technology companies founded by its members. But now the old hackers couldn't swap tips and code anymore; too many of them had corporate secrets to protect. The Homebrew club eventually disbanded in 1986.

People with home computers were now dialling up to the internet using modems attached to their PCs. They exchanged emails and joined mailing lists. Many people also became active on bulletin board systems, or BBSs. BBSs enabled users to dial into a specific server and exchange files or messages with other people. Computer hackers could swap information and software without having to meet face to face. This new ability to connect fostered the creation of hacker groups such as the Legion of Doom in the United States and the Chaos Computer Club in Germany. The new breed of hackers hung out on BBSs and formed into small groups. Many still tinkered with hardware, but software became the primary focus for many. They worked on hacking new code and programs, and the internet made it relatively easy for them to share their creations with others. Hackers in different parts of the world were getting connected.

The original hackers had been instrumental in establishing and developing the computer industry and the internet, but now they and their inventions had become increasingly corporate. Still, the new class of hackers in the 1980s did share one obsession with their predecessors: the telephone system. They recognized that it was the door that could lead them inside large corporations and government agencies. Inspired by the phone phreaks of the 1970s, they pushed the envelope even further. They sought access to the most powerful machines and networks in order to learn more about computers. But the social and legal environment had changed. Law enforcement was now aware, and wary, of hackers and hacking, as were other components of society. This was in part thanks to Hollywood.

The 1983 hit film *WarGames* told the story of a young computer hacker who unwittingly breaks into the Pentagon and almost causes World War III. While the phone phreaks had attracted their fair share of media attention and law enforcement scrutiny in the 1970s, *WarGames* awoke North American society to the supposedly catastrophic results that hacking could bring about. Hackers went from being the unsung heroes of the computer age to being painted as dangerous vandals. The image of the pimply-faced teenage hacker who brings down society was in large part because of *WarGames*. It was then reinforced that same year when a group of teenagers was discovered to have hacked its way into the computers at the Los Alamos National Laboratory, a nuclear research facility, as well as into more than fifty other computers.

In 1986, U.S. Congress passed the Computer Fraud and Abuse Act, making it a crime to break into computer systems. Undeterred by the new law, hackers continued their push into forbidden areas. Hackers in West Germany broke into computers in the United States; a graduate student at Cornell University unleashed a worm over ARPANET that infected thousands of computers. At the same time, the internet was rapidly expanding. By 1989, more than eighty thousand computers were connected.

Near the end of the decade, Kevin Mitnick earned notoriety after he was given a one-year prison sentence for computer fraud. Mitnick used social engineering to get past a guard at MCI, a telephone company, and steal manuals that gave him the secrets of the system. He was also convicted of stealing software from Digital Equipment Corporation. The concept of the hacker-as-criminal was being firmly planted in the minds of the public and law enforcement, who were beginning to wonder how far these clever miscreants would go.

For many, the answer appeared to come on January 15, 1990, when the entire AT&T phone system crashed. It stayed down for nine hours. Almost right away, the company and law enforcement suspected it was the work of hackers. A law enforcement initiative based in Arizona, dubbed Operation Sundevil, soon went into action to target the hacker underground. Even the Secret Service was involved. Operation Sundevil is often cited as an investigation into the AT&T failure, but it also targeted credit card thieves who worked online. It was part of a larger crackdown on illegal hacking activities in the United States. In early May 1990, arrests were made in fourteen U.S. cities. Included in the arrests were people the Secret Service and others viewed as criminal hackers. They ranged from people allegedly involved in credit card theft and illegal access to computer systems, to those who had been running BBSs and even an online publication.

The FBI proudly declared that hackers could no longer hide behind the "relative anonymity of their computer terminals." Yet in the end, hardly any indictments were served. As for AT&T's system?

A bug in its own software had caused the crash. No matter. The FBI and other agencies had become focused on the dangers that hackers posed. The result was the 1990 crackdown. The lines were drawn. Hackers weren't welcome in polite society.

The 1990s saw many more famous incidents of hacking. Kevin Poulsen, now a respected writer on computer-security issues, was a hacking prodigy in the early half of the decade. He used the handle "Dark Dante" and became famous, along with two other hackers, for rigging phone lines to win a Porsche in a Los Angeles radio contest.

After going underground to hide from the FBI, he eventually pleaded guilty to seven counts of mail, wire, and computer fraud; money laundering; and obstruction of justice. Poulsen was sentenced to fifty-one months in prison and paid US$56,000 in restitution. The same year he pleaded guilty, a sixteen-year-old hacker named Richard Pryce, who used the handle "Datastream Cowboy," was arrested for breaking into computers housed at the Korean Atomic Energy Research Institute, Griffiths Air Force Base, and NASA. Poulsen and others earned a measure of fame, but the FBI was about to capture the man who would become the most famous hacker of all.

Early in the morning on February 15, 1995, FBI agents entered an apartment building in Raleigh, North Carolina, and banged on an apartment door, demanding to be let in. Inside sat Kevin Mitnick, now thirty-two years old. After serving his sentence, he had returned to his old ways. Mitnick had begun his career by hacking away on computers in Radio Shack stores. Now he was a fugitive from the FBI. With this arrest, he was about to become the first mainstream hacker celebrity.

"A convicted computer felon on the run from Federal law enforcement officials since November 1992, Mr. Mitnick has used his sophisticated skills over the years to worm his way into many of the nation's telephone and cellular telephone networks and vandalize government, corporate and university computer systems," read a *New York Times* article published the day of his arrest. "Most recently, he had become a suspect in a rash of break-ins on the global Internet computer network."

Mitnick became a hacker celebrity during his time on the run. In the end, he would spend four years in jail for his crimes, though many of the accusations levelled at him by law enforcement would prove to be bogus. (Among them, the allegation that he had stolen twenty thousand credit card numbers and hacked into NORAD.)

In addition to the highly publicized capture of Mitnick, 1995 also saw the launch of a remarkable new internet technology, the World Wide Web. It was the system that enabled the internet to become home to websites, images, and video—the things most people today associate with the internet. (People often think, erroneously, that the internet and web are the same thing. The internet is the underlying network of connected computers, while the World Wide Web is a system that runs on top of the internet and supports websites, hyperlinks, and other content.)

Amid the arrests and advancements of 1995, Hollywood once again devoted a film to hackers and hacking. It was called simply *Hackers.* For many young, aspiring hackers such as me, it opened our eyes to what was possible with computers and the internet. More specifically, it confirmed to me that computers and hacking were destined to be my life, not just a hobby.

"It's almost a biological thing," said Steven Levy in *The Secret History of Hacking.* "People are hard wired to be hackers or not to be hackers. You can see it in kids. Some kids just take to computers saying, 'Oh my God, this is the way I can finally express this part of myself.'"

That was me. I believed I had been born to hack.

CHAPTER SEVEN

The Birth
of Archangel Michael

IT WAS AGONIZING to have to wait for the file to download.

I'd finally located a pirated copy of *Hackers,* a film I absolutely had to see. Now I was staring at my computer screen as the film slowly downloaded over my dial-up internet connection. I could easily have gone to see it in the theatre, but I wanted to flex my warez-finding skills and get my own copy for free. I thought that was how a real hacker would do it.

When the file was finally on my hard drive, I rushed to open it and then sat back to watch Hollywood's take on hackers. I can still recite most of that film line by line, but my all-time favourite scene is where Dave, a.k.a. Crash Override, a.k.a. Zero Cool, takes over a TV station using a combination of computer skills and social engineering.

At one point in the film, Dave looks up from his computer and grabs the phone. He dials a TV station and pretends to be an employee who needs access to the computer network in order to retrieve a file. The hapless security guard assists him by reading out the phone number on a modem. Within seconds, Dave hacks his way inside the station's system and replaces the show currently on the air with an episode of *The Outer Limits*.

It was thrilling for me to see a Hollywood film dedicated to hackers and hacking. (The fact that it starred Angelina Jolie also caught my attention.) Hackers were now heroes on the big screen! I felt it validated all the time I had been spending online. People were waking up to the influence of hackers in the new, connected world.

By the time *Hackers* came out, I was eleven years old and already obsessed with the world of hacking. That film, and my interactions with people online, inspired me to reach higher, to try to become a real hacker.

AOL, once my main territory for testing tools and attacks, now seemed like child's play. Nobody who was serious about the internet used AOL. In the hacker community, it was seen as a joke because the service was so basic. In fact, it wasn't the real internet. It served you AOL content and kept you in AOL chat rooms. It was like a wading pool, while the internet was an ocean. AOL was sanitized and, for the most part, calm. The internet was wide open and at times turbulent. I was drawn to the rougher parts of the internet. Watching Dave take over a TV station showed me what an elite hacker could do. Messing around on AOL simply wouldn't cut it anymore.

I realized what I was missing with AOL when I discovered the world of BBSs, bulletin board systems. In essence, they are simply places where you can chat with users, upload and download software and other files, and read news. But BBSs were home to a much savvier brand of user. They were often run by an internet service provider or educational institution. There were lots of them out there, each with their own following and user group.

When I started using BBSs, I came across computer games and applications that were sold in stores but had been cracked so that anyone could now use them free of charge. I wanted to grab as many as I could, but many of the BBSs worked with a credit system: You were required to upload data and applications to earn enough credits to allow you to then download items. Typically, for every one kilobyte (one-thousandth of a megabyte) uploaded, you were awarded three kilobytes for downloading. You needed to have things to offer in order to reap the benefits. Another way to take advantage of a BBS was to get to know the system operator, since he or she could give you a high-credit account. But because I had nothing to upload, system operators weren't interested in talking to me.

Even though I was moving away from AOL, I managed to locate a channel there for trading BBS information. People were offering BBS accounts with unlimited downloads or high credit, but no one was willing to give either to me as I had nothing to offer in return. I needed to upload cracked software and games in order to be able to download others. But how could I get my hands on this stuff if I couldn't first download it?

That's when someone on the channel told me about a chat network called IRC (internet relay chat). The many layers of the internet were slowly being peeled away for me. BBSs and IRC were known to many serious internet users, but I was still just a kid trying to find my way, so it was tremendously exciting whenever I discovered another one of these networks.

I found mIRC, an application to let me connect to IRC, and immediately started looking for warez channels. I needed to get my hands on things I could upload to BBSs. The results were astonishing. I discovered a world of users looking for the same thing I was: pirated software. I found channels distributing applications, games, music, and pornography. Again, however, there was a barrier. The high demand for pirated software combined with a limited amount of bandwidth resulted in long user queues. I needed to hop the queue. I decided to become friends with channel owners and chat with them on a regular basis. I needed to build up my reputation with them so I could avoid the lineups. But after spending a short time trying to ingratiate myself, I realized that I would get nowhere.

I eventually found my way to another network within IRC, EFnet. It had well over fifty chat channels dedicated to pirated software and other illegal activity. But I still had the same issue with queues as before. The problem was clear: I didn't really know anybody online, yet everything was built on relationships and reputation. I needed to find a community where I could acquire these things. I realized that it was key to maintain a consistent online identity: People needed to know they were chatting to the same person from day to day. But a lot of people had similar chat handles, so I needed something original. And it had to be cool.

I became Archangel on EFnet, and also occasionally Arkangel if someone else had already taken the first. I was named after the Archangel Michael. My family isn't very religious, but I did take First Communion and also had confirmation. I liked the name because it was mine, only a little more serious.

My goal was to find a channel where I could become a member in good standing. A place to hang out and get my hands on warez. I noticed some channels were looking for new members and decided to focus on one called #WarezIWC. It turned out that it was recruiting hackers to breach computer networks. Once a network was compromised, the group would store its warez on it.

By hanging out in #WarezIWC for a while, I learned an important fact about the internet: The places with the biggest networks and largest amounts of bandwidth were educational facilities, such as universities, and big businesses. Universities were #WarezIWC's preferred target because, unlike major corporations, they didn't have the resources to properly monitor and protect their networks at the time.

A single person on a slow dial-up connection couldn't act as a download point for warez—it would take too long for people to get their pirated software. Warez needed to be hidden on one of the big bandwidth centres' networks. Then you could tell your crew where the stash was and everyone could upload and download at will.

When the legendary bank robber Willie Sutton was asked why he robbed banks, he reportedly said, "Because that's where the money is." Hackers broke into academic and corporate networks because that's where the bandwidth was. On the internet, bandwidth is currency. It's also power.

I wanted badly to join IWC, a hacker crew, and learn how to break into networks. It sounded like fun. It also sounded like these were the kind of people I had been seeking out since first being punted off AOL. IWC was a crew of hackers. They stuck together and worked together. I had been working solo for more than two years and was frustrated by my lack of progress. I wanted to find somewhere I could belong. Again, though, I had nothing to offer IWC. I was just a kid who had used simple hacking tools to cause trouble on AOL. I didn't have any skills, and I didn't have any warez. I was of no use to them. But I wasn't going to let that stop me.

I messaged the owner of the channel, who went by the name Drakus, to tell him I wanted to be a member of the group. I asked him to help me learn how to obtain access to computers without permission. He replied he was looking for people who *already* knew how to do that. Kiddies need not apply. In other words, bug off, noob.

Instead of taking the rejection to heart, I decided to be persistent in order to show Drakus my level of commitment. I messaged him again and again, telling him I was serious, that I could learn quickly, that I was dedicated. He eventually relented

and decided to start me with basic training to see how quickly
I could learn. Depending on the results, he said, I could become
a member. I finally had a chance to prove myself.

Drakus invited me into a private chat room populated with
members of IWC and a few other recruits. I received a private
message from him giving me the rundown on the network,
which channels not to create problems in, and the hackers and
crews to watch out for. At first, I had no idea what he was talking
about. I was there to learn, so why was he warning me off so
many things? Was it really that dangerous? I thought that IRC
was a chat network with some underground pirating, nothing
more sinister than that. I was completely naive.

Drakus showed me that there were people online with the
power to shut down computers, erase data, build malicious tools,
steal personal information, disrupt credit ratings, and much more.
All of this from behind a computer. Yet another layer had been
peeled back, and I was more excited than frightened. AOHell
suddenly seemed so far away, so simple and stupid. This was the
real deal. Real hackers, real danger. Real power.

Drakus told me to install Linux, an open source operating
system, on my computer if I wanted to advance faster. I was being
put to the test to see if I could handle a more complex operating
system. My DOS experience helped me navigate my way, and
I soon had Linux up and running on my computer. Now Drakus
wanted to see if I could run some simple attacks.

I felt one step closer to my dream of becoming a hacker.

AS EVERY COMPUTER USER KNOWS, all commercial software
has bugs. These are flaws or faults within the software code that
can cause errors, such as the famous Windows "blue screen of
death." Bugs are hugely important to hackers. By discovering
holes and bugs in popular software applications, hackers can find

ways to exploit them and gain access to computers running that software. Computer companies constantly work to patch holes and fix bugs before hackers can create "exploits" for them. It's a constant struggle. Often, the hackers are one step ahead, shooting in and out of holes before companies and network administrators can patch them up.

Drakus told me that he wanted to see if I could run some of these so-called exploits in order to gain access to high-bandwidth networks. The goal was to gain root access—like the pass-key to a specific computer on a network, or even to the entire network. You would run an exploit, which itself was a piece of code or an application, to attack a specific vulnerability. Then, ideally, you would gain root access.

I was given the exploit program and began trolling the net for vulnerable networks. I was in a sense walking through backyards with a crowbar, checking to see if there were any doors or windows that it would fit into. (An exploit is usually a little more elegant than a crowbar, but the result is the same: access.) I soon discovered other, smaller programs that I could use to quickly scan for vulnerable networks. This saved me a lot of time.

I ran the network scans and then launched the exploit when I found a good target. When everything worked well, I'd walk away with root access, the Holy Grail. If the server I compromised was tied to a network with a huge amount of bandwidth, I had done a great thing for the group. I did this endlessly, spending most of the night running scans and executing exploits. I demonstrated to Drakus that I was committed and could perform well on these basic tests. I still wasn't coding anything or devising new attacks, but I had already learned much more than I had ever known about how the internet works—and what its weaknesses were.

I progressed quickly and earned respect within IWC, which resulted in me being established as a member only one week after being recruited. With that status, I dedicated even more time to the group. I viewed this as serious work and began ignoring my homework and worrying less about school. I'd rush to get my homework done on the bus each morning on the way to school. My grades slipped a little but not enough to trigger any alarms. I didn't care as much about art or science or history—I cared about the future. As far as I was concerned, that was the internet.

By the time I was in grade five, there was also a computer at my mom's house, though I wasn't allowed free rein with it: After I had spent a few solid days working away on it, my mother and stepfather told me I wasn't allowed to use it as much. The final straw came when they discovered me on it very late one night. They saw how I could easily spend an entire day and night on it, and they thought it wasn't healthy. They let me use the computer only every once in a while, which was very frustrating for me.

Even with restricted access to a computer, it didn't take long for me to climb the IWC ladder. I had a strong resolve to become a respected hacker. I loved having challenges placed in front of me. I soon realized I needed to gain programming skills if I was to advance and truly become a hacker. I read books on C programming, Perl programming, computer networking, and anything else I could find. With this knowledge, I wrote simple applications to run on my computer. These were tests to see if I could write a program that actually worked. I wrote a program to keep track of all my hockey cards, a simple tool that allowed me to search by year and company. It worked. I was ecstatic. One more hurdle was being overcome.

In the meantime, I worked to become friends with other hackers and establish Archangel as a known name on IRC. It was a slow process. Most hackers didn't want anything to do with people they didn't know. As I slowly earned the trust of other hackers, I gradually obtained more code and applications, which helped make me a bigger threat. I began gaining credibility with other hackers. I was also invited into discussions in private channels.

My desire for status and recognition weren't the result of being deprived of attention at home or at school. I had a loving family and lots of friends. People often think of young hackers as loners with few social skills, but that wasn't true of me. I had even changed schools so that I might get involved in more extracurricular activities.

Up until the age of eleven, I had attended private school. But after complaining to my mother about the lack of extracurricular activities at the school, she agreed to let me attend Sunnydale, a large public school, for grade six. Sunnydale was a big change for me. I was excited at the prospect of being around more kids and having access to a range of sports teams and activities. I believed public school was going to open up a whole new world for me.

My mother drove me to the school on a beautiful, sunny September day.

"Have fun, it's your first day of school," she said after noticing how nervous and excited I was.

I kissed her on the cheek, then made my way to the playground. Kids were running around. My first impression was that public school was open and free. There was no dress code, no demand that we try to behave as though we weren't kids. I stood outside for a few minutes looking for a way to join in, but I didn't know a single person. I headed inside to find my classroom, hoping that new friends weren't far off. My plan was to pick my desk and see who sat around me, but the room was already almost full. I had to grab one of the few remaining spots and hope for the best. The boy at the desk next to mine looked up with a braces-filled grin as soon as I sat down.

"Hey, I'm Nick," he said. "I've never seen you before; are you new here?"

"Yeah," I said. "It's my first day. My name is Michael."

The teacher announced that she would give the class thirty minutes to talk and catch up with one another before starting the lesson. Nick began asking me about sports. Then I felt a tap on my shoulder and turned around to see a skinny kid with a big smile on his face.

"Hey, do you play football?" he asked.

"Yeah, I play all sports," I told him.

He told me his name was Brian and that he played football with a group of kids at lunch, which was exactly what I wanted to hear. I had come to public school so that I could play more sports and ditch the stuffy private-school uniform. Now I seemed to have made two new friends on the first day, Nick and Brian. I was already feeling great about my decision to switch schools.

Over the course of the year, Nick, Brian, and I became best friends. We lived within a five-minute bike ride of one another and spent nearly every day together. I wasn't some loner staying indoors all the time. The three of us rode our bikes in the woods and played football and basketball. I also discovered that Nick and I had something special in common: computers.

Just about everyone played video games, but we shared a love for anything to do with computers. Nick was the only friend who understood them. When we weren't off playing sports or riding our bikes, Nick and I hunkered down in front of whatever computer we could find. We also connected because we both had older brothers whom we idolized. I had Lorenzo; Nick had Phil. We thought our brothers were the coolest kids in the world and tried to act and dress like them.

A small patch of woods separated my house from Nick's. Our routine was to meet in the middle of the woods and then head to one of our houses. At Nick's house, his mother inevitably offered us food and drinks. She was one of the nicest people I've ever met. His father, a dentist, was at work most of the time, but he was just as kind and welcoming as his wife. Nick's family was always happy to see me, and my parents felt the same way about him. He was a polite, friendly kid.

Aside from my family, Nick and Brian were the most important people in my life.

In grade seven, because of our love of computers, Nick and I took the only computer class available to us—typing. It was boring and easy, but all we cared about was having access to computers. Nick was as fascinated with them as I was. Typing was the only way to get our computer fix at school. We couldn't wait to take more computer classes together as we made our way through high school. We also saw how our older brothers ruled the school, and Nick and I talked about the day it would be our turn.

Even though Nick and I shared a lot of information about computers, he never really knew what I was up to when I spent weekends at my dad's house. My time alone on the computer was sacred to me. I kept my growing obsession with hacking a secret from everyone, including Nick. When I first discovered AOL, the internet had just been another part of my life. Slowly, though, it was taking over.

Just as any young kid wants to be seen as cool by people at school, I wanted the same thing online. I was ambitious: My goal was to make sure my name echoed in the hacking community forever. I wanted my handle to be part of the discussion about the top hackers in IRC. I knew it would be a difficult goal to achieve, but I had never wanted anything more in my life.

It often seemed nearly impossible to obtain the knowledge and status of some of the elite hackers. Still, I didn't give up. My mind was on hacking all day and all night, no matter where I was. I'd often find my mind wandering in class, wondering if I would come home to discover a disaster on IRC, with all my networks compromised and me kicked out of my hacking group. Every second I spent away from my computer meant I wasn't there to keep learning, or to protect myself against attacks.

Plenty of people were better than I was at hacking, and they could have done serious damage to the work I had done. They could attack my computer and wipe it clean of all data, or discover my real name and cause problems for me in the offline world. They could find the networks I had compromised and lock me out of them. I was advancing, but I wasn't what you would call an "elite" hacker.

My life away from the computer was still important enough that I wasn't ready to sacrifice it in order to achieve my goals as a hacker. But that was all about to change.

CHAPTER EIGHT

Blindspot

MELISSA, A SCHOOL FRIEND, was on the other end of the phone line, but I couldn't understand what she was saying. I pressed the phone to my ear to try to hear her better. Melissa's words were mixed with sobs and crying so that it was almost impossible to understand her. I could make out one word: *Nick.* She kept repeating it.

"Nick ... Nick ... Nick ... Oh God ... Nick ..."

"Calm down, Melissa," I said, "calm down. What happened?"

She took a few seconds to regain her composure.

"Nick ... Nick died," she said.

"Is this some kind of sick joke?" I yelled back. "'Cause seriously, I'm not laughing."

"No, Michael, it's not a joke, he got hit by a car," she said and then began sobbing again.

I fell backward onto my bed. The phone was at my ear, but I could no longer hear Melissa. Everything was blank, silent. A terrible sadness flowed through my body. As it engulfed me, I tried to ward it off by convincing myself this was all a joke. Then I heard the beeping in my ear. Call waiting. I hoped someone was calling to tell me not to believe Melissa. I switched to the other line.

"Yo, man, what the fuck, have you heard?" came Brian's voice. He was filled with adrenalin. Melissa could hardly get out her words, but Brian was practically yelling at me. He sounded out of control. At that moment I knew it wasn't a joke. I connected us on a three-way call and they told me what had happened.

Nick had been at his neighbour's house, playing in the driveway. Snowplows had cleared the streets from a recent storm, leaving high snowbanks on the sides of the road and creating blindspots. Nick had run to the end of the driveway; an oncoming car was driving by at the exact moment he stepped onto the street. The driver never saw Nick coming.

I was twelve years old and my best friend had just died. I had never before lost anyone close to me. I couldn't understand how Nick could suddenly be gone when everyone else was still here. I told my mother, and she was devastated by the news. She loved Nick. Everyone loved Nick. That night, the local evening news confirmed everything I had been told. Nick really was dead.

The next day, everyone at school knew what had happened. I still clung to a faint hope that it was all a tragic mistake. I tried to convince myself that Nick might walk through the classroom door at any moment. Because we were best friends, people kept coming up to Brian and me to talk about Nick. They wanted to connect with him through us, but I felt I had nothing to offer them.

The school organized a meeting with a grief counsellor to help Nick's friends deal with the shock of his loss. Brian and I showed up to find a large number of people in the room. I didn't see how all these people could have been affected by Nick's death. I thought they were faking their sadness just to miss class. I scoured the room to see who there had actually known Nick, who really cared about him. I decided that most of the kids had no business being there. I was racked with sadness, but anger took over as I sat listening to people who didn't know Nick talk about how hard his death was for them. Brian and I, his best friends, were silent as the others went on and on. I wanted to scream, "Fuck you! None of you were even friends with him! Get the fuck out of here!"

Everything about the situation enraged me. I didn't feel those kids had a right to grieve. In my mind, only a handful of us really knew and cared about Nick. The rest of them had no idea what we'd lost. I had moved past denial and was now completely entrenched in the anger stage of grief. The meeting was making me feel ill. While my schoolmates spoke, I bottled up my emotions and focused on the fact that Nick was never coming back, which just made me more upset.

After school, I went over to Nick's house. I wanted badly to see his family, yet I dreaded coming face to face with his mother. How was it possible that she had just lost her youngest child? I felt as though all the emotions I had bottled up at school were about to come pouring out. I didn't want to burden her with my feelings.

Nick's mother opened the front door with tears streaming down her cheeks. She managed to smile at me as she led me inside. Even though her twelve-year-old son had just been killed, she didn't want *me* to be sad. We sat down and she explained what had happened, but soon the both of us were crying, and she was telling me how much Nick had loved me. I loved him too, I told her.

Brian and I were asked to be pallbearers at Nick's funeral. After the service at the synagogue, we helped carry Nick's casket to a hearse and followed the others to the cemetery. I had never been to a Jewish funeral before and had no idea that it was traditional for people to take turns shovelling in soil once the casket has been lowered into the ground. The thud of dirt and rocks hitting the top of the casket was jarring. Nothing has ever sounded louder to me. Nick was disappearing right before my eyes. He was never coming back.

I felt broken. Not just my heart but every part of me—my physical body and my mind—felt beaten up and broken. I didn't see how anything was going to be the same in my life, or the world around me. I tried praying at night for help, for Nick to come back, for me to feel normal again. It felt futile. Nothing was going to change what had happened.

Nick will always be a part of me. To this day, Brian and I visit his grave on the anniversary of his death. I've gone at other times as well and have seen his mother there. I always make sure to tell her that Brian and I will never forget Nick. Each time I see her, I'm conscious of the fact that I've grown older, something Nick never had the chance to do. The only thing I pray for now is that I get the chance to see him again when I die.

THE LOSS OF NICK meant I no longer had a close friend who shared my fascination with computers. As a result, my online life became even more separated from my offline world. School was not the same without Nick, and I started to care less about classes and grades. Computers and the internet became my hideaway, the place I went to escape the loss of Nick. My quest to become a hacker now became a full-fledged obsession. I pulled back from school and friends and plunged deeper into the hacking community.

The anger and grief I felt over Nick's death left me with a blindspot; I didn't see that I was trying to lose myself online. As a result, the more I advanced with computers and the internet, the worse things got in the offline world. My grades began to slip and I earned a reputation as a troublemaker. I had always made excellent grades in math, but the other subjects bored me. I just didn't see any point to them. I started talking back to teachers, throwing erasers during class—doing anything to pass the time and stave off boredom. I didn't realize it at the time, but I was lashing out in anger at the loss of Nick. We had met and become friends through school. With him gone, school fell lower on my list of priorities. I felt I had found a new crew of friends online in the form of Drakus and others at IWC and on IRC. Brian and I remained tight, but I knew I was pulling away from what I saw as my former carefree life.

I now believed IRC was where I belonged. It was also a place where I could vent some of my anger. When I talked back in school, the teacher disciplined me. If it got really bad, my parents got involved. Although I was aware of the dangers on IRC, I didn't have to conform to as many rules as I did offline, or worry about what my parents would do to me. I let my mouth run freely in online channels and began attempting more and more attacks. It was a classic case of an adolescent acting out after experiencing a major personal loss. The difference was that I was doing it primarily online.

The Archangel was now out for vengeance.

CHAPTER NINE

Call Me Mafiaboy

ONE DAY WHEN I WAS IN GRADE EIGHT, I came home to discover that one of my worst fears had been realized.

I entered the IWC channel to meet up with Drakus and the others, but he was nowhere to be found. Several days passed with no sign of Drakus. The other IWC members and I began getting worried. What had happened to our leader? This was where the virtual nature of the internet became frustrating. I didn't have a phone number or address for him. I didn't even know his real name. After so much time spent working together and hanging out online, he had suddenly vanished. I had no way of finding out what had happened to him. No one in IWC knew what to do. After a few weeks, we decided it was best to disband; the backbone of our group was gone. And if someone could knock Drakus offline, maybe it was best for us all to move on and cut our ties with him.

That was the day I became something of a mercenary. I was solo. I had no protection, no group. The loss of Drakus and IWC wasn't nearly as devastating to me as Nick's death was, but it reinforced the idea that I would always have to fend for myself. People wouldn't always be around, so I had to take care of my own problems. Nick's death had sent me deeper on my quest to become a hacker, and the disappearance of Drakus had the same effect.

Hacking wasn't a switch I could just flick off. I had much more to learn, and I wasn't going to let this setback derail my ambitions. I wanted to be the best and resolved that nothing was going to hold me back. I spent the next few months learning more about programming and networking, and compromising more networks. I soon realized that hacking without a crew doesn't make a whole lot of sense because you limit your resources and knowledge base. I wasn't able to message someone I could trust and ask for his or her input or advice. I needed to find my way back into a crew.

The only way I was going to get recruited to one of the elite groups was to make a name for myself. And I knew of only one way to make this happen: war. I would have to put my most powerful networks to use against known hackers and groups in order to get recognized. I had never set out to launch a major attack on anyone before, and the fact that it had to be directed at people with skills was frightening. If I failed and lost the networks under my control, I would be finished as Archangel. Everyone would know I got "owned." It was a risky proposition, but I felt as though I was becoming a real hacker, that I could take on larger groups on my own. This was a critical juncture for me. Either I would succeed and find my way into a more advanced crew, or I would fail and be back at square one.

I decided to aim high right away and launched an attack aimed at taking over #exceed, the biggest channel on EFnet. It had roughly three thousand regular members. The channel was maintained by a long-serving hacking group known as Madcrew.

Taking over a channel could be easy, but it depended on how quickly and powerfully you could attack it. It also depended on how careful the owners were. In any channel you can see who the owners (known as the operators) are because an @ symbol precedes their names. The more operators in a channel, the harder it is to take it over. Most times, a handle with an @ symbol is actually a computer on a different network that has been hacked and then set up to act as an operator. Such a computer is called a bot, as in robot. No one is sitting in front of it telling it what to do. It has been hacked and installed with bot code that sets it up to automatically act as an operator in the channel.

To take over #exceed, I scanned all of the operators to see if any of the computers had a weakness I could exploit. Once I found at least one, I ran a program I had found called Hunter to hijack that computer's connection. Then I instructed it to give operator status to my personal network of bots, which were usually university-owned servers I had compromised. With my own bots now set up as operators in the channel, I worked quickly to take operator status away from all of the previous owner's bots. My network of bots was large enough that I was able to knock all of Madcrew out of the channel. It was a fast attack and my palms were sweating the entire time. Would there be a counterattack I hadn't planned on? Something I didn't know about? I was nervous up until the last of Madcrew's operators were booted out. It was over in just a few minutes. The channel's log of operators confirmed that Madcrew's had been removed.

After I took over #exceed, I changed the topic message in the chat channel to let everyone there know that I had just owned Madcrew. The channel was mine. Archangel had struck. That takeover caused a lot of griping from people on IRC. People didn't like the fact that I took on a reputable crew. Some thought I was pushing my luck, but I managed to hold on to it for a while and prove my status.

I was so pleased with myself that I continued to war with other known hacking groups. The only way to get status and recognition was to take people out. I dedicated myself to it and soon felt I had a talent for building networks ("botnets") and launching channel takeovers. But not all my attacks were successful. I suffered damage by having some of my botnets temporarily shut down when people launched low-level denial-of-service (DoS) attacks to knock me offline.

In a DoS attack, you bombard someone with an avalanche of server requests until his or her network is paralyzed. It's as if you've sent so many people rushing into a small building that no one can get in or out. After a while, no one can even move. When that happens, a network is effectively shut down. I took note of the effectiveness of this attack. I had heard of it before—it was like punting on steroids, so it appealed to me—and decided to learn more about it. I needed to add DoS to my repertoire.

At the end of what I considered to be my personal crusade, I had twelve channels under my control and had compromised three hacking crews. I was pleased with the results. But had anyone noticed? Would I forever be on my own?

Finally, the call came. One of the bigger groups, known as Alpha, approached me. Its members had heard about me and were impressed with my work. I was invited to join and accepted. I was officially a member of Alpha. I once again had a crew. Best of all, I had done it on my own.

Alpha was much more established than IWC. It had fourteen members and six major channels under its control. It was exactly what I was looking for, and I quickly proved my worth by taking out rival hacking groups that posed a threat to us. The other members were also helpful in improving my skills. They taught me new things about computers, networking, and hacking, and gave me access to their private exploits. I had more knowledge and tools than ever before. I also had status.

By now I was thirteen years old. In the past seven years I had gone from being a six year old learning DOS commands and playing games to being a hacker with status in one of the better groups on IRC. It was the biggest achievement of my young life, and I didn't hesitate to flaunt it online. When I joined channels populated with hackers chatting, instantly someone would say, "He's a member of Alpha." Then everyone knew who I was. It was like walking around in gang colours. People moved out of the way. They treated you with respect. They feared you.

I moved around online with a new-found swagger. My kiddie days were over. This was a huge transition for me, and I decided it was time for me to send the Archangel to heaven. That handle had served me well for years, but it was linked to my days as a kiddie. I didn't want that label following me around. I began thinking up new handles for myself but nothing stuck. Then one day I logged on to my computer and went online, as usual, but, without realizing it, I was operating under a different handle. My brother had used my computer to download music under an alias: Mafiaboy. I liked it as soon as I saw it. *Mafiaboy*. I remember staring at the letters.

At that moment, I decided it would be my new identity. I loved gangster movies and thought Mafiaboy sounded cool and intimidating, the kind of name you'd have if you were in a gang. It was a fuck-the-world name, which was how I sometimes felt after Nick's death. I was determined to make a fresh start with Mafiaboy. Lorenzo had already created an account on a Montreal ISP with the email address, so I created another email address with the name at a different service provider.

I just had one last thing to do in order to solidify my new name. I logged on and notified my crew: Call me Mafiaboy.

Archangel was dead. Long live Mafiaboy.

CHAPTER TEN

I'm TNT

"YOU'LL NEVER make anything of yourself."

I remember sitting in the principal's office in grade nine when he said those words. At that moment, I realized school was never going to work for me. My grades and behaviour had declined since Nick's death in grade seven, but hearing my whole future written off caused me to completely give up. My school life just fell apart. The teachers and principal had made their minds up about me, and I had given them plenty of reasons to do so. I decided to embrace the fact that no one expected anything good from me. I'm a problem? I'm a troublemaker? Fine, then why not act like one?

Grade nine was a turning point for me. I cared less and less about what people thought of me at school. It was easier to keep getting worse than to turn things around. The whole process of school seemed pointless. I believed I was going to make my name with computers and hacking and didn't care about trivia like what the capital of Portugal was. Let the other students learn that. I already knew what I wanted to be. I knew one day I'd show everyone what I was truly capable of.

During my grade nine year, I was suspended several times for bad behaviour and poor grades in every class except for math. As a result, I was asked to leave Lindsay Place High School. On the last day of school I was play fighting in the hallway with a friend when a teacher walked by and mistakenly thought we were fighting for real. I was sent to the principal's office, and he told me that was my third strike. Go find another school, troublemaker.

I was happy to be gone from there and enrolled in Riverdale High School for grade ten. By that time, my mother was at a loss for what to do with me. She finally agreed to let me go live with my dad. Lorenzo had moved there a few months earlier and I was excited to go. Aside from being back with my brother, and the more lenient environment, the change meant I would finally have total access to a computer. I could achieve the things I had always wanted to do. I spent the summer of 1999 learning as much as I could and compromising as many computers and networks as possible.

EARLY THAT SUMMER I broke into the network belonging to Outlawnet Inc., an ISP in Oregon. To me it seemed to be just another network I had managed to compromise. But I later learned Outlawnet was operated by students at Sisters High School. They built and maintained their ISP as a group project. The kids spent time maintaining servers, dealing with customers, and learning about the internet. It was the kind of project I would have loved to have been a part of at school.

As Dan Verton details in his book *The Hacker Diaries: Confessions of Teenage Hackers,* which contains a detailed retelling of the incident at Sisters High School and the subsequent investigation into my case, just after noon on Tuesday, June 8, students attempted to log on to one of their servers and discovered they were locked out. At first the students thought the server had crashed, but they soon realized it was more than a crash. Some of them ran to find Jon Renner, the teacher in charge of the ISP. Renner discovered that the main server was inaccessible and files had been deleted.

I had found my way onto their network and taken over one of their servers. I remember that particular server because I had used it constantly that summer. It was reasonably powerful and also allowed me to spoof my IP address: I could route myself through Outlawnet, then enter an IRC chat room and make it appear as if my connection originated at fbi.gov or some other address. I used that server to help cover my tracks, but at a certain point I realized it contained logs of my activities. I wiped it clean to protect myself. It was likely a short time after that that the students realized something was wrong with their server. (I rarely wiped out a server I had compromised, as this in itself would draw attention.)

On June 14, the FBI stepped in to work on the case. Renner handed over the logs of the compromised server, and agents began the lengthy task of analyzing traffic that had flowed in and out of the server. It was as if they were following a trail of footprints in the snow. By following them back to their origin, the FBI hoped to find the source of the attack, the person responsible.

This was difficult and time consuming. I had burrowed my way into Outlawnet's network through a series of compromised computers. The FBI had multiple sets of footprints to follow, and it would take them until December to see that the attack had originated in Canada. That month, the FBI contacted Marc Gosselin, a corporal with the Royal Canadian Mounted Police. The FBI told him they had tracked the source of the attack back to the network belonging to Sprint Canada. Using a warrant, Corporal Gosselin obtained information from Sprint Canada and followed the trail to an ISP in Montreal, Delphi Supernet. He discovered that the account he was interested in had been suspended months earlier by the ISP because the account owner was suspected of hacking. Although the account was inactive, Corporal Gosselin was able to obtain information about who had owned the account.

"Gosselin had narrowed down the source of the attack to a two-story, sea-foam-green and brick mansion-like house on Rue du Golf [sic] ..." reports author Dan Verton.

The Sisters trail led Corporal Gosselin to my father's house. Because of the lack of evidence, he wasn't able to close the Sisters case. But the connection between our house, the suspended account, and Sisters gave the FBI enough reason to call my father and make him aware of the activities taking place in his home. The problem with the FBI's strategy was that the ensuing phone call struck my father as strange and lacking credibility. He had no idea what hacking was and didn't believe that the kids in his house were capable of it. My dad knows a lot about business, but he doesn't touch computers. This is how he recalls the exchange, which took place sometime in 1999:

"Can we speak to Mr. Calce please?"

"Yes, speaking," my father said.

"We are authorities from the United States ..."

"What does this have to do with me?"

"We would like to inform you about some activity in your household."

"What activity is that?"

"We have reason to believe there is hacking activity going on in your household."

"Hacking? What?"

"Someone is using a computer to obtain illegal unauthorized access to sensitive networks."

"I'm sorry, but I barely know how to use computers and there is no one here that would be capable of that," my father said. "This must be some kind of a mistake."

"We are currently making an investigation."

"That's fine, you can go ahead and make an investigation. I have my young boys here who just play games, and myself," he said. "You must have made a mistake. Thanks, have a nice day."

Then he hung up. My father didn't know what to do. After thinking about it, he decided it was time to cancel the dial-up internet account in our house. I was upset with his decision, especially because he didn't offer a specific reason for why he was doing so. But I already had access to a few stolen internet accounts, so I just used those instead. It was business as usual for me because I had no idea the RCMP and FBI had come so close to catching me.

At that point, the Sisters investigation was filed away. Corporal Gosselin and his FBI counterparts didn't know it at the time, but the investigation into that incident, dubbed Operation Claymore, would eventually lead them back to our house a few months later in the hunt for Mafiaboy.

RIVERDALE HIGH SCHOOL was a new setting, but the outcome was the same. I soon earned the same reputation I had had at Lindsay Place, and my behaviour didn't change. I continued to be a terror in class, with the exception of computer class. While the other kids were learning basic programming languages such as Pascal, I was writing out programs in C, a more advanced language. The teacher saw how hard I worked on my own and encouraged me to keep at it. That was the only class I made any effort in. Outside school, I played basketball on the weekends, hung out with friends, and continued to stay up into the early hours working online. It was, for me, a perfect blend of typical teenage life and online skulking.

At fifteen years old I felt as though I had already attained many of my online goals. Mafiaboy was a known entity on EFnet; I had compromised hundreds, if not thousands, of computers on large networks; written several of my own applications; and maintained several IRC channels.

I was happy to lead two lives. The so-called real world of people was still important to me, but it was dwarfed by the significance of the internet. That shift in priorities was my secret. Online, I felt unencumbered by rules, parents, or preconceptions about age and ability. I had worked on my own to establish Mafiaboy, to make him a force on IRC. He was me, but he was also my creation. It was as if we were two people. There was Michael Calce, loyal son, friend, and brother. A fifteen year old who loved hockey and basketball and hanging out with friends. Then there was Mafiaboy, the mysterious, dangerous EFnet hacker who owned channels, compromised networks, and could knock you offline at a moment's notice.

I had comic book–like fantasies about my secret identity, about protecting it from discovery by the people who knew me as Michael Calce. If the two were ever linked, I knew it would mean the end of Mafiaboy. I'd be punted offline—this time permanently—by my parents. That would be an embarrassing, inauspicious end to the daring hacker known as Mafiaboy.

Meanwhile, I had once again managed to move up the ladder in the EFnet hacking community. I had attracted the attention of a different, more elite hacking crew and had left Alpha behind. I was now part of TNT/PHORCE, one of the most notorious groups on IRC. It was a private, invitation-only group. One of the things that attracted TNT/PHORCE to me was what some call my packet power. Packets are the small bundles of information that data are broken into in order to move over the internet. I had so many compromised computers on big networks that I wielded a significant amount of bandwidth. I could easily marshal my bandwidth to attack a channel or an individual.

TNT wanted me, and it also wanted my networks. I was ecstatic to be invited into the group. This was the IRC equivalent of being drafted by the Montreal Canadiens or the New York

Yankees. The group maintained #shells, an IRC channel that was well known among hackers. Holding control of that channel gave you major status. It showed you had juice, power.

I was perhaps the youngest member of TNT, though none of the other members knew my real identity. Nor did I know theirs—they went by names such as Phifli, Adpro, str69er (a.k.a. str), Jedi, Mshadow, and tabi. Like any good organization, we had a command structure and everyone filled a role. Some were expert coders. They built applications and exploits and were, in effect, the research and development or intelligence arm of the group. Others, like me, specialized in compromising networks and testing and refining the tools. We were the soldiers.

One of the biggest misconceptions about me to this day is that I didn't know how to write code. I did. I'd even done some coding for a friend of my father's who owned a technology company. But I'm the first to admit it wasn't my specialty. Other people, such as str69er, were much better at it than I was. But I often took their code and made changes to it after I had tested it out. I wasn't just blindly grabbing tools and exploits and booting them up—I had to understand how they worked in order to be able to use and then refine them.

In fact, code was the universal language of TNT. It had to be—many of our members were Russian. English wasn't always understood. When together in a channel, we spoke in a mix of networking and internet terminology, chat shorthand, and snippets of code. And, yeah, trash talk. Inevitably, a group like that has some pretty big egos. The main IRC channels where hackers hung out were mostly filled with boasting, trash talk, insults, and vulgar language. You did the real work on private channels with people you trusted. Those big channels were for talking shit, and I admit to being a major participant. I felt emboldened by my status with TNT and the power that came with it. I knew there were other serious groups and hackers out there, but I felt we were the best—that I was one of the best. I didn't hesitate to let others know it.

In retrospect, I was pretty mouthy online. It was an easy thing to do from behind a computer, especially since I knew I had a lot of bandwidth and a solid crew backing me up. TNT was like a family in that we looked out for and helped each other. But we were also structured like a military unit. People needed to respect rank and know their role. Each member of the TNT/PHORCE crew had different strengths and weaknesses. Together, we were a formidable group.

The TNT/PHORCE Crew

Str69er (a.k.a. str)—One of the leaders of TNT. He was a Russian who spoke broken English and spent his time coding as opposed to launching attacks. He mostly kept to himself and didn't communicate with people he didn't know. But if any of us needed help with coding, he would be the guy to step up. Str69er was generous about sharing his private botpack code with the group. This was the code that enabled someone to maintain a network of bots. Str69er was also a member of the #!adm channel, one of the most hardcore exploit groups. Its members came up with many of the exploits used by people on EFnet. It meant we always had the latest exploits to use in the hunt for new networks to compromise.

Dreamwalker—A founder of TNT, he was the least active member, occasionally popping up to make decisions. Then he'd disappear again. Also Russian, Dreamwalker spoke little English and rarely interacted with anyone other than the Russians in the crew.

Adpro (a.k.a. proda)—A leader and the crew's day-to-day manager. He had the power to recruit new members and kick out existing ones, though he rarely did the latter. Adpro was relaxed and diplomatic. He was also our treasurer, except instead of money he kept shells—the hacked accounts we had obtained on various networks. Adpro was often the one who made the final call on which EFnet channels or users to attack. He saw attacks as a last resort and often attempted to talk operators into handing over a channel to avoid war. Occasionally, the diplomatic approach worked. (I preferred when it didn't.)

Jedi—A soldier with a total disregard for rules or boundaries, which meant he was often my partner in crime. Like me, Jedi was a foot soldier with a lot of packet power. He was less of a loudmouth than I was but was easily offended by outsiders and non-TNT members. If somebody said or did something to piss him off, it was on: He would start loading up his botnets and launch an attack. Jedi wasn't afraid of anyone. I think he was from Florida, but I never knew for sure.

Mshadow—One of the few non-hackers in TNT. Mshadow managed to join because he had great personal relationships on EFnet. Just about every group and major network operator knew him. That meant he could be useful in using his connections to get people booted off IRC or banned from certain networks. He was usually pretty calm, but he was always asking personal questions, which I found suspicious. That's likely how he managed to get to know so many people. Still, he knew Mafiaboy; Michael was none of his business.

Phifli (a.k.a. Mikey)—A serious coder. Phifli didn't bother with the battles; he was all about writing code. At my urging, he would go on to write Trinoo, a denial-of-service tool that was a key inspiration to me when I began working toward my series of major attacks. Although he didn't engage in battle, Phifli loved taking over channels. And he was kind enough to let his fellow TNT members test out his tools. That gave us a big advantage.

Venial—Not an official member, but he hung out with us and helped out with takeovers. In my opinion, he was one of the best hackers on EFnet, in terms of warfare. Venial was capable of launching large DoS attacks and taking out hacker groups by himself. We often worked together on takeovers and got along well. Venial had a low tolerance for boasters and was quick to pull out the big guns and shoot if someone offended him or questioned his abilities.

Atomic—The only TNT member I can recall getting kicked out of the crew. From what I heard, he leaked information to another hacker group. Adpro found out and booted him from TNT. The whole affair was kept quiet even within our crew, and no one asked too many questions—it was Adpro's call to make.

tabi—A member who was another non-hacker. She was the TNT drama queen. Tabi didn't mess with any of the battles, but she played an important role by maintaining phorce.net. That site was the CNN of EFnet hacking: If you took over a channel or owned another user, the information would go up there. Hackers loved to make the front page of phorce.net. Tabi was energetic and brought a sense of humour to the group. Her messages always ended with a smiling emoticon, but she wasn't afraid to flaunt her TNT colours to other groups. This often resulted in battles. I frequently got messages from her saying something like, "Mafffia, guys are bothering me in #vanity ☹ help plz." So I'd then go into #vanity and boot people or take it over. I was often her protector, which was fine by me.

EFNET WAS FILLED WITH CREWS BIG AND SMALL, and there were also a lot of independent hackers floating around causing trouble. Many of the old school on EFnet looked at us as a bunch of reckless kids causing trouble. But TNT members ranged widely in age, and we were far from alone when it came to battling and talking trash. EFnet was filled with people launching DoS attacks, stealing each other's handles, and trading shell accounts and warez. This is the community I was a part of. Some people don't consider what we did to be real hacking. Everyone has their opinion, but I know how much work I and others put into learning how to program and penetrate systems.

There was a large community of hackers on EFnet, and some of them did things that shocked even me. For instance, they might infiltrate a rival hacker's computer and networks and post that hacker's personal information on phorce.net. You'd see somebody's real name, family details, social security number, banking information, even vehicle registration, up on phorce.net. When you got hit it could be devastating—and then it would end up on phorce.net for all to see. Even though the battles and arguments took place online, there could be offline consequences.

I wasn't always as careful as I should have been, but I never ended up humiliated on phorce.net or owned by another hacker. I did get recognition on phorce.net, however, for taking over channels. That made me proud, but it also made me arrogant. I started feeling invincible, as though I had one underground part of the internet within my grasp. That's a dangerous amount of power to think you have, especially at an age when you simply aren't mature enough to see the larger issues at play.

Laws and consequences never entered my mind. I was on a dangerous path.

I was wholly obsessed with the battles raging between the different groups on EFnet. I barely had any time to sleep. A channel could easily be taken over if I left it unprotected or didn't have one of my fellow TNT members watching over it. That was the nightmare I was constantly trying to avoid. I often thought of what happened to Drakus, the way he just disappeared.

The constant conflict between hacking crews on EFnet meant people were always working to come up with new exploits and attacks—you needed to innovate in order to maintain your status. One of the most common areas of innovation was denial-of-service attacks, which had grown to become my preferred method of attack.

DoS attacks had already existed for years in the form of tools such as WinNuke, Teardrop, and BMB. WinNuke arrived in 1997 as a way of taking out a computer or server running Windows 95, Windows NT, or an earlier version of the Windows operating system. It would leave your target with the infamous "blue screen of death." Basically, you shut the target's computer down and forced him or her to reboot. It was a more advanced version of punting. Early DoS tools had the effect of knocking people offline by bombarding them with huge amounts of data until their systems shut down.

Simple applications such as WinNuke worked only on Windows targets, which was limiting. The people hanging around on EFnet weren't everyday users running Windows 95; they were running Linux or other UNIX-based systems, which were more complex—and more secure—than Windows. That's why, years before, Drakus had made me start out by installing Linux on my computer. If I wasn't able to handle that, I had no business even thinking about being a hacker.

By the late 1990s, it seemed as though a new DoS tool was being released on a monthly basis. As soon as a new DoS tool came out, somebody would develop one that was even more sophisticated and harder to defend against. Tools such as Smurf, Slice, Stream, and other programs came along. They were more advanced and enabled you to take down bigger targets, as opposed to just one computer or server. Hackers used these tools every day to shut each other down and demonstrate who had more power. This was where my packet power came into play. I had enough bandwidth and servers under my control that I wasn't in danger of being taken out. The same was true for TNT as a whole. We were well protected, but that could change at any moment. A coder could create a new attack and we would have been at a significant disadvantage. It was, in effect, an arms race. We were trying to see whose missile could go further faster, and carry a more damaging payload. Instead of warheads, we were using packets. It was a matter of who had the most bandwidth, the most servers, and the best software to use in attacks.

These battles dominated my life. The stakes seemed so much higher than what I scored on a history test, or whether my basketball team won a game. Those things were increasingly trivial, but I had to keep up appearances. If my parents knew what I was up to online, they'd cut off my internet access.

Even though DoS tools were readily available to many people, launching a DoS attack is not as easy as it sounds. There are many variables to take into account, such as routers, filters, firewalls, ports, and bandwidth. You had to prepare the best possible attack based on the target you were after. You couldn't just load an application and expect to take out somebody with skills and networks. It took knowledge, planning, and proper execution. I worked hard at these things and learned with each new attack I launched.

In 1999, Phifli, a fellow TNT member, released a new DoS tool. It was called Trinoo and it was a beast. It had the potential to shift the power base on IRC. I had encouraged him to work on a new tool that could increase the intensity of a DoS attack, while also making it easier to launch and control.

After Phifli provided me with Trinoo, I loaded it up on approximately 150 networks and tested it out on rival groups and hackers. The results were more than impressive. I was able to shut down thirty servers on high-bandwidth networks in a matter of minutes. Because of my existing networks and the way I customized Trinoo, I became even more powerful. I took down servers and hijacked channels. This made me a big target, and the same was true of TNT as a whole. Other crews worked to use Trinoo in the same way. The arms race intensified.

Hacker groups were now making alliances in an attempt to thwart TNT and take us out. At one point we saw that another major crew, Core, was being decimated. By the time the attacks on them were finished, Core had lost all of its channels and was forced to disband. Once that happened, we swooped in and recruited their best members. One such member went by the name T3. He was a botmaster or botherder—someone who is talented at maintaining bot networks. Adpro approached him and T3 came on board.

I was somewhat suspicious of T3, and not just because he had come from a rival crew. He often asked me questions that I felt were too personal. How old was I? Where did I live? He and Mshadow always seemed a little too curious about my true identity. I also found him extremely arrogant, too much even for my taste. T3 had skills, but he didn't want to hear what other TNT members had to say about coding or maintaining botnets. Several months after he joined, I engaged in an online discussion with him, Mshadow, and Swinger, another member of TNT, that would later come back to haunt me. I should have remained suspicious and kept my distance from both Mshadow and T3, but my mouth eventually got the better of me, as usual.

AS THE BATTLES RAGED ON IRC, a more advanced form of DoS attack began to emerge. It used more sophisticated packets (SYN packets) that made it even harder to trace the origin of the attack. I had never really worried all that much about being tracked after launching a DoS attack. In fact, I often wanted people to know it was me who had hit them. That was the way to send a message to rival crews. Now, though, you could hit someone and back off into the shadows. It made already reckless people, including me, bolder.

Because of the new DoS attacks, things were escalating at a fast pace. We had picked up more members and continued to expand, but other groups were forming alliances to come after us. It was difficult for me to protect my networks and our crew's channels while also launching attacks. Because of this reality, I began thinking about a strategy to simplify the launch of a DoS attack. With that simplification would also come a greater impact. Trinoo had ushered in an era of distributed denial-of-service (DDoS) attacks, the ability to launch a coordinated attack from a variety of networks. I was now thinking along the lines of a mass distributed denial-of-service (MDDoS) attack. Trinoo on steroids.

In basic terms, my goal was to chain my large network of servers together so that I could easily launch one massive attack. Rather than having to launch a separate attack from each server, I wanted to be able to centralize and make them work as one. This would heighten the impact and also save me a lot of time. The idea was to have one so-called master, and multiple slaves, or "zombies"— the term used to describe compromised computers and servers that have been linked together in a vast network, or botnet.

I wanted to create the most powerful DDoS tool anyone had ever seen. I knew what I wanted to build but also recognized that I needed to work with someone who had better coding skills than I did. The project would go faster, and I'd be able to learn from him or her in the process. Suddenly, I was the one doing the recruiting.

I got in touch with Sinkhole, the best DoS tool coder I knew. He had written Slice, a popular DoS tool, and I knew he was the perfect man for the job. We chatted online and I laid out my plan. He agreed to help code the tool but stressed that he wanted no part of infiltrating computer networks. He loved the challenge of creating a new application but had no interest in using it. I wanted to build it *and* use it. We agreed to keep our plans secret. I didn't even tell my fellow TNT members. With Sinkhole on board, I believed I would soon have the means to put an end to the DoS arms race.

Sinkhole created an account for me on his computer and we used a tool called TTYSnoop that enabled me to watch in real time as he coded. He did the vast majority of coding, and I chimed in with edits and suggestions. As the program progressed, I took it out for little test drives on EFnet. This meant attacking people and seeing how many of their servers I could shut down at once. People noticed I had a powerful new toy. I started getting messages from other hackers who had questions about what I was doing. Mainly, though, they wanted the code.

At least fifty hackers must have begged me to leak the code and give them access to the tool, or at least to shut down certain targets on their behalf. The requests didn't stop—I constantly had hackers messaging me. But I turned them all down. This was my secret project. I wasn't about to use it to settle other people's disputes.

At the same time as Sinkhole was refining the code, I worked to increase my networks of compromised computers. As impressive as the tool looked, it couldn't change the balance of power on its own. I needed to build the largest possible network of compromised computers. The more bandwidth at my disposal, the greater the impact of the attack.

I decided to build three networks using different applications in order to see which would be the most powerful when combined with Sinkhole's application. One network was built using Barbed Wire, another used a tool called tf2k, and the last one was connected with a tool I created and named Zilch. (In the end, each of these networks had more than two hundred compromised computers. It took me a lot of sleepless nights to get there.)

I soon felt as though I was running out of time. The war on EFnet was getting out of control. People battled for hours to take over channels. There was such a constant onslaught of packets that it seemed as if no one knew who was attacking whom anymore. Even TNT was beginning to get mowed down by opposing groups. This brought a new-found sense of urgency to my secret project.

In late 1999, I decided to focus my efforts on hacking computers connected to American universities. Their huge bandwidth and lax security made them natural targets. I infiltrated Harvard, Duke, Purdue, Columbia, UC Santa Barbara, University of Miami, University of Texas, Berkeley, and UCLA, among many others. After two months of building my networks, I decided I needed to do a test to see which ones would work the best against TNT's rivals on IRC. To do this, I would need to find a different class of target. Something big and well protected.

Because of my previous tests with Trinoo, I knew that small corporate or university networks would instantly crumble in the face of my new, more forceful attack. That wasn't what I wanted. I needed to go up against a major network to see how powerful

each of my three networks really was. Then I could use that information to perfect my attacks on IRC. This was new territory for
me. Although I had for years been compromising computers
on various networks, I had never launched an attack at a major,
well-known target. But I was convinced the only way to test my
new tools and networks was to aim big. Otherwise, I wouldn't get
the results I needed. After some research, I saw that a search engine
would be my best target because it deals with a huge amount of
internet traffic. At the time, Yahoo! was the world's top search
engine.

It was now early February 2000. I combined close to half of
my total networks and worked to link them together for a major
test. I slept little, ignored school, and kept my plans to myself. Not
even Sinkhole had any idea what I was planning, let alone anyone
else. I decided my secret project now needed a name. Because it
was aimed to create chaos on IRC, I called it Rivolta, which
means "uprising" in Italian.

I knew that if my tests were successful, I'd have the necessary
power to finish off the hacking crews slowly chipping away at
TNT's dominance. My uprising would become a full-fledged
revolution that could change the power structure on IRC for
good.

But before that could happen, Yahoo! would need to get hit.

CHAPTER ELEVEN

Rivolta: The Attacks

FEBRUARY 7, 2000, was a Monday. A school day.

I normally hated getting up in the morning for school because I was usually up until 2 or 3 A.M. working on Rivolta and chatting on IRC. That day, however, I was up early and making final preparations for my strike against Yahoo!. This wasn't going to be just another of my typical attacks against a fellow hacker. I had therefore programmed everything to launch while I was away from the computer. That way, I thought, I could say I was at school if other hackers—or the police— asked me about it. But the truth is that I expected the Yahoo! attack to fail. My idea was to see how Yahoo! defended itself and then adapt and improve my plans. I knew I had created something powerful but had no idea of its true force. I planned to come home, read the logs of what happened, and then make changes so my real targets couldn't beat me back.

In retrospect, I see that I had no clue as to the potential impact of what I was doing. At the time, Yahoo! had one of the biggest websites and networks on the web. It was also a multibillion-dollar company that was seen as a bellwether of the technology industry. The dot-com boom was still in force, and Yahoo! was one of the biggest success stories. I should have seen that any kind of attack against Yahoo! would have been big news, even if it failed. But those factors didn't register in my mind. I had built something remarkably powerful and wanted to put it to the test. I was a kid with a new toy.

I made my final preparations and headed to school, already contemplating what I might discover when I returned home.

TESTIFYING AT A CONGRESSIONAL HEARING in Washington in June 1991, computer security expert and author Winn Schwartau said, "Our computers are so poorly protected they can essentially be considered defenceless. An electronic Pearl Harbor is waiting to happen."

Since that moment, the threat of a large-scale electronic attack had become a focus for defence and information experts. A July 1995 *Washington Post* article about terrorists or other enemies using cyberwarfare to attack the United States' information infra- structure was headlined "The Pentagon's New Nightmare: An Electronic Pearl Harbor." Two years later, Deputy Secretary of Defense John Hamre testified at a congressional hearing. "We're facing the possibility of an electronic Pearl Harbor," he said. "There is going to be an electronic attack on this country some time in the future."

Those warnings were largely specific to national defence, but the internet had grown to such an extent that by 1999 it was an integral part of the U.S. economy. An attack on major e-commerce giants could have a significant effect on the economy. The internet was woven into every facet of life in North America and around the world. People were beginning to upload their personal information and details about other aspects of their lives. They were banking online, doing business online, living their lives online. If something happened to show that some of the largest and most respected internet companies were vulnerable to attack, consumers could lose confidence in the internet and begin to pull back. This could have major economic repercussions.

But these realities were far from my mind as I planned Rivolta. What fifteen year old thinks about the economic interests of the United States? I had an innovative new attack I wanted to unleash on IRC, and naively decided to venture out from the cover of that part of the internet to test my capabilities. I had no intention of claiming the Yahoo! attack as my own. As I say, I thought I could run my test, learn what worked and what didn't, and move on with my plans. If someone came asking, I would say I was at school during the attack. It seemed like a reasonable plan at the time.

Needless to say, I was wrong.

Yahoo!, one of the Web's biggest information portals and e-commerce sites, was completely caught by surprise. The initial flood of data packets overwhelmed one of Yahoo!'s main routers at speeds higher than 1 gigabit per second, the equivalent of more than 3.5 million average email messages every minute P.M. ...

This was a highly distributed attack that used many computers as pawns, better known as zombies, in the attack. And a highly sophisticated hacker or group of hackers was likely responsible, according to Yahoo! experts who were doing battle with the attackers ...

"It seemed the attacker(s) knew about our topology and planned this large scale attack in advance," wrote a Yahoo! system administrator a few days after the initial flood of packets took down the Yahoo! network. "It seems that this is definitely a DDoS attack, with attacker(s) [who are] smart and above your average script-kiddie."

—Dan Verton, The Hacker Diaries

AT 10 A.M., I WAS IN SCHOOL, AS PLANNED. I moved from class to class, my thoughts fixed on the attack. Along with planning the time of the attack for ten o'clock, I had programmed a series of tests to run in the background. These would enable me to see how Yahoo! was affected, how it defended itself, and what the overall results were. More than anything, I was excited to pore over the data and get back to work on my bigger plans. It never occurred to me that while I was sitting in class, system administrators at Yahoo! would be frantically trying to keep their sites and network online and accessible to the millions of people who visited them every day. Having never expected that result, I floated through the school day as chaos erupted in Yahoo!'s offices.

According to media reports, Yahoo! began experiencing serious problems at about 1 P.M. EST that day. Soon after that, its website began to grind to a halt. People typing "yahoo.com" in their web browsers were largely unable to access the site. Others were unable to access their free Yahoo! email accounts. Yahoo! was being hit with a barrage of packets emanating from multiple places—just as I had intended. This was a distributed denial-of-service attack on a massive scale. It qualified as a mass distributed denial-of-service (MDDoS) attack.

"Monday's [Yahoo!] failure drew renewed attention to the risks facing the fledgling world of electronic commerce, where hackers can shut down even the largest online stores," reported the Associated Press on February 7. "It basically says nobody is safe, if Yahoo! can be taken down with all the resources behind them," Elias Levy, chief technology officer at SecurityFocus.com, a respected computer security website, told the Associated Press.

Arriving home just before 4 P.M., I discovered that Yahoo! had been knocked offline. In fact, I was unable to access its website. It was still down! I sat in front of my monitor, frozen in a state of shock. This was not at all what I had expected. I combed through my reports to see what had happened. It almost seemed too easy.

I had expected to fail and learn from that experience. But Yahoo!, one of the giants of the internet, had seemingly crumbled due to my attack.

Although Yahoo! was back at full strength within the hour, its failure had raised a question in my mind: Was my attack that good or were Yahoo!'s defences that poor? Some experts believed it was the latter.

"It's kind of silly it took so long [to defeat the attack]," James M. Atkinson, president and senior engineer at Granite Island Group, an internet security consultancy, told the Associated Press. "The fact [the attack] went on for hours indicates a management and infrastructure problem that does not involve technology. This should have taken [Yahoo!] off the map for fifteen to twenty minutes, thirty at the most."

Meanwhile, the National Infrastructure Protection Center issued a statement saying that it was "highly concerned about the scale and significance of these reports."

I wasn't reading any of the media reports. I didn't usually watch the news or read newspapers. The news sources I cared most about were phorce.net and the community of people who populated the hacking channels on IRC. As the mainstream press and computer security community engaged in speculation about what had happened, I logged on to IRC to see what my peers thought.

I wasn't surprised to see the Yahoo! attack generating a huge amount of chatter, but it was funny to see other people claiming credit for it. Even someone in the private TNT chat room stepped up and said it was he who had launched the attack. I thought this wasn't such a bad thing and was happy to let others face scrutiny for now. (Although many subsequent media reports claim I boasted about taking down Yahoo.com that night, I don't recall doing so.)

I felt overwhelmed by what had happened, what I'd achieved. I couldn't help but see it as an achievement. I felt as though the huge amount of bandwidth under my control was now coursing through my veins, as if I now embodied the networks I controlled. I lay relatively low on IRC that night and didn't do much work on Rivolta. The entire experience was so draining that I crashed and went to bed early for the first time in months.

I WOKE UP EARLY THE NEXT MORNING and immediately went to my computer. That was when I learned somebody had hit Buy.com with a similar type of attack. To this day there is speculation that I was responsible for the Buy.com attack, but I wasn't. I learned about it after it happened. That attack coincided with Buy.com's initial public offering and seemed aimed at hurting its stock price on the first day it hit the market. I never had any desire to inflict financial damage, though I acknowledge the attacks I orchestrated had that effect.

As I learned more about the Buy.com attack, I began to feel as though someone out there was challenging me, suggesting that anyone could do what I had done to Yahoo!. I took it as a message to me. Armed with what I now knew was an incredibly powerful botnet, and still feeling the rush of power from my Yahoo! attack, I resolved to answer back. It now seemed like a game, a contest. But instead of warring face to face on IRC, I was engaged in a fight where the battlefield was as public as it could get. It was as if a back alley fight had made its way into a shopping mall, causing people and businesses to flee for cover. By taking up this challenge, I was further exposing myself to law enforcement and the public, and that could only mean more scrutiny, more trouble for me. Instead of waiting to set up my next test as planned, I immediately set upon a new target: eBay.

I launched the attack late in the afternoon of February 8. This time I was behind the computer, watching in real time. eBay fell harder and faster than Yahoo!; it seemed to be only a matter of minutes before the site was crippled. People who had been tracking or bidding on auctions were unable to access the site. I saw how easily eBay went down and didn't prolong the attack. I had proven my point and, more importantly, gathered more information about the power of my networks.

Satisfied with what I had accomplished, I entered the #shells channel to see what hackers were saying. A part of me wanted to stay silent, but I also thought that perhaps I could scare some of the other hacking groups if they saw that I, a member of TNT, had taken out Yahoo! and eBay. I didn't realize it, but I was moving beyond my initial goal of testing out my networks. My plans were changing: Instead of launching a direct attack on rival groups, I thought it would be just as effective to admit responsibility for these attacks and prove what I was capable of. Maybe they would back off if they saw it had been me.

I decided to ease into the discussion. No one would believe me if I simply wrote that I was responsible. Lots of people were doing that. So I asked everyone who they thought had the most powerful networks. Who couldn't get taken down?

Many people in the channel knew me and that I had DDoS capabilities, but no one seemed to think it was me behind these serious attacks. One person suggested CNN would be impossible to bring down because of its advanced networks, its huge traffic numbers, and the fact that it also hosted a large number of other websites.

Okay, I thought, CNN it is.

I set to work targeting CNN and in just minutes launched the attack. I waited until the site was almost completely down, then went back into the channel.

"Check CNN," I said.

I watched as a string of expletive-laced messages filled the channel. People were freaking out. I had sent my message: Anybody thinking about fucking with TNT or me had better back off. I had taken out CNN at a moment's notice. The sense of power I felt was overwhelming. It was also addictive. I didn't want to stop there—this was my *rivolta,* the moment I could seize to make my name resonate on IRC forever.

ONE COMMON THEME in many of the films and comics I enjoyed in my offline life is that someone who is essentially good, or at least benign, can lose control and their sense of self when they acquire a great amount of power. In comics, it might be a superpower. Someone who used to walk among his or her peers learns to fly and gradually becomes drunk with power. Or in a film, a good soldier, for instance, may go rogue after getting his hands on a fantastic new weapon or critical piece of intelligence. The message, of course, is that power corrupts. We are human and frail; we can be manipulated and lured by the promise of fame or fortune.

Ever since punting my first user on AOL years before, I had been on a mission to acquire online knowledge and power. By taking down CNN and letting people on IRC know it was me, I had created the exact moment I had dreamed about for years. It was no fluke—I had worked long and hard to get there. Like Dr. Frankenstein proclaiming "It's alive!" this was my moment of triumph.

Armed with my new-found sense of power, I fell into the trap of thinking I was untouchable. In order to achieve what I had always wanted, I lost a bit of myself and all sense of right and wrong. I was obsessed with making Mafiaboy a legend on IRC for all time.

After the people on IRC saw that CNN was down, I pushed for another suggestion. *Test me. Let me show you what I can do.* I wanted desperately to be known and recognized, and also to be feared. Although I felt in total command of my abilities, I had in reality lost all control.

Amazon.com was next. Yahoo! had worked better than I had imagined, but it had taken time to bring its network down. eBay and CNN had both fallen rather easily. Amazon.com? It was even more of a joke. I had kept the attack on CNN going for close to two hours, but Amazon.com fell so hard, so fast, that I took mercy on it. It was like a hamster on a wheel was running its network. I kept the site down for about an hour, then called it off. I felt like a Rottweiler mauling a Maltese.

I had been challenged to take out CNN.com and Amazon.com, and I did in a matter of minutes. I had made my point. It was getting late in the evening and, just like the previous night, I was exhausted from both the adrenalin and the work. The hundreds of servers on networks all over the United States and in other countries that I had used were also probably feeling overworked. They had for hours been firing off packets at a furious pace. I resolved to rest my networks, and myself.

I lay down in bed but wasn't able to sleep. Had I really come this far? I'd gone from phishing and punting on AOL to launching massive denial-of-service attacks that had taken down some of the internet's biggest websites. I was fifteen years old and had done it from my bedroom in my father's house while the rest of the family moved around in other rooms, oblivious. As I thought about the attacks, I began wondering what was going on in the channels on IRC. How could I sleep when this was the biggest day of my life?

I logged back on to IRC and saw that the chatter hadn't stopped. Different people from before were now online, and I had received something close to eighty messages, some from people I didn't know, asking me if it was really me who had done the attacks. Some had heard from others that I was behind the attacks. I didn't bother answering because I had already provided the proof to the hackers on IRC. It didn't occur to me that the FBI and others would soon use that same proof to track me down.

I stayed online for most of the night, watching the chatter scroll by on my screen. My botnets had performed far beyond expectations, but I still hadn't used all of my resources. One network had yet to be tested. In a haze of sleep and ego, I decided to do one more attack. I had already gone so far that one more seemed inconsequential. Damage had already been done, so why not complete my final test?

E★TRADE was my target. I directed my untested network to hit the site, then waited to see if I would get the same results as before. E★TRADE was seriously crippled by my attack. I held it down for just over an hour before shuffling over to my bed. It was around 7 A.M. and I would need to be up soon for school.

"MYSTERY DEEPENS as hackers attack more high-profile Web sites," reported the Associated Press on February 9, 2000:

> Hackers stepped up a three-day electronic assault Wednesday against some of the Web's most popular sites, inconveniencing millions of Internet users and deepening the mystery of the attackers' identities. The apparently coordinated campaign spread to E*Trade, ZDNet and other flagship sites.
>
> The growing anxiety about the Internet's vulnerability contributed to a broad selloff on Wall Street and even prompted efforts by top federal officials to reassure Americans that authorities were doing all in their power to combat the online vandalism.

"We are committed in every way possible to tracking those who are responsible," Attorney General Janet Reno, the nation's top law enforcer, said in a news conference in Washington.

On February 9 I arrived home from school to discover that a copycat hacker had hit technology-news site ZDNet.com and another online trading site, Datek.com. As with Buy.com, I had nothing to do with these attacks, but many people thought the same group of hackers was responsible. For the record, I still have no idea who went after Buy.com, ZDNet.com, and Datek.com.

The copycat attacks meant little to me. I had achieved my larger goal of testing my networks. I also managed to instill fear among rival groups on IRC. But I wasn't satisfied. The rush of power I had felt the night before was still present. So too were the rival groups. The real goals of Rivolta had not been achieved. I was hell-bent on pushing ahead.

I now knew what I had under my control. TNT's enemies were going to face the consequences. Over the next week or so, I launched attack after attack on IRC, taking out multiple targets at once, seizing control of major channels and knocking enemies offline. In the midst of my assault on IRC, I received a message from Adpro, one of the leaders of TNT. He knew I was the one behind the attacks on CNN.com and yahoo.com. He had a request.

"Bring Dell to its knees," he said.

Adpro was the one who had recruited me into TNT. He was also what you might call one of the generals of the group. He was a leader, but he wasn't a warmonger. Indeed, Adpro was often the voice of reason within TNT. When somebody wanted to declare war on another group or launch a takeover of a specific channel, Adpro would be the one to calm people down. He looked for solutions, not destruction. Although he must have had a reason to want to bring down Dell, I didn't feel it was my place to ask what it was.

"No problem," I told him.

On February 12, I attacked Dell.com. As with the others, the site began experiencing problems almost immediately. I kept the pressure on for a couple of hours, then ended the attack. Adpro was happy and thanked me for the work. Interestingly, Dell didn't publicly acknowledge the attack until after it was contacted by the FBI. By that time, I was focused on ending the IRC battles. Attacking sites such as Dell.com wasn't my priority; I had done it only to help out a friend. I went back on IRC and proceeded to plant the Mafiaboy and TNT flag everywhere I could. This was my final assault, what I considered to be my true triumph. I would still refer to what I had done to CNN, E★TRADE, Amazon, and Yahoo! when in IRC channels, but it was the war in IRC that consumed me the most.

I now felt I had forever established myself on IRC. Whether people believed I was behind the attacks on the websites was beside the point. They knew what I had done on IRC. That was the goal all along. In roughly a week of testing and execution, I had achieved it.

I thought the name Mafiaboy would live on forever. In an unexpected way, I was right.

CHAPTER TWELVE

Wanted: Mafiaboy

MY BIG, STUPID mouth.

When I look back at what caused the FBI and RCMP to suspect me for the attacks, I can't help but think of my mouth. Since grade seven, it had been working overtime in class, online, everywhere. Whether it was telling a teacher to shut up or inciting conflict on IRC through taunts in a chat channel, my mouth had long been one of the most active parts of my body. In the end, it helped ensure I was held accountable for my actions.

I often let my networks and attacks do the talking online. That was the case with the attack against yahoo.com and the others that followed. But then I followed up my actions with reckless bragging in #shells.

Aside from the hubris that drove me to keep up the attacks, there was my general love of trash talk. From behind my computer, no one knew I was a skinny fifteen year old hacking from inside my father's house. I projected the idea that I was ten feet tall, a menace, a badass. Your worst nightmare online. I created that image partly by my actions and partly by my words. By accepting the challenge to hit CNN and then following up with E★TRADE, I made a direct link between the channel trash talk and real-world actions. I had implicated Mafiaboy in those attacks and, by extension, in the attacks against Yahoo! and eBay.

I naively didn't think that making claims in IRC was dangerous. Everybody talked shit on IRC. The difference was that I had talked shit and then backed it up with devastating attacks on e-commerce giants. There were witnesses. Hell, there was even a transcript. Anyone could have saved that chat and passed it on to the authorities.

It turned out that wasn't necessary. The FBI already had an agent posing as a hacker on IRC. He was sitting at a computer as the conversation about CNN scrolled by.

My big, stupid mouth.

IN 1999, William "Bill" Swallow, then an investigator with the U.S. Department of Defense, was sent by the Pentagon to work in the FBI's computer intrusion squad in Los Angeles. Swallow's early career had been dominated by conventional investigative work, but his facility with computers eventually helped him become a top Pentagon information security specialist. Not long after he took on that role at the FBI, Swallow, along with other agents, was drafted to help hunt the international hackers who had launched attacks against NATO's information systems in late May 1999.

In the wake of NATO bombing campaigns against Serb positions in Kosovo, hackers from Serbia, China, Russia, and even the United States attacked NATO servers housed in Brussels. The attacks, which were spurred by a NATO bomb that hit the Chinese embassy in Kosovo, managed to take NATO's web servers offline. It hampered the alliance's ability to communicate with the world via its website. More importantly, it awoke the world to the reality that international conflicts would also now be fought online.

"In an electronic assault on NATO's presence in cyberspace, computer users in Serbia managed to temporarily disable the alliance's site on the World Wide Web last weekend and cause intermittent outages over the last few days," reported *The New York Times* on April 1, 1999. "Paul Magis, NATO's web master, said computer hackers bombarded the site in what is known as a 'ping attack,' which twists a protocol that Internet computers use to query one another into a weapon that overloads a server with more queries than it can handle simultaneously."

The online attacks against NATO continued over the following weeks, as did other attempts to breach the network security of the Pentagon and White House. By late April, the FBI had seen enough China-based attacks on the U.S. information infrastructure to issue a public advisory. "Hackers already have unlawfully defaced a number of U.S. Web sites, replacing existing content with pro-Chinese or anti-U.S. rhetoric," according to an April 28 *New York Times* report headlined "F.B.I. Warns That Chinese May Disrupt U.S. Web Sites."

Swallow was a key member of the FBI team assembled in Los Angeles to help thwart and investigate cyber attacks against U.S. government information systems. The team was managed by Charles Neal, the head of the Los Angeles field office, who had previously led the case against legendary hacker Kevin Mitnick. It also included Jill Knesek, a programmer and investigator who had worked at the Naval Satellite Operations Center. She too had been involved in the Mitnick case. It was an FBI information security all-star team.

Their work was greatly aided by Swallow's sources in the Serbian hacker community. According to Dan Verton in *The Hacker Diaries*, "One was a U.S.-based hacker who had close ties to the Serbian hacker underground, as well as family members still in Serbia. The other source was located in Kosovo and was a former war hero who had been working with the Serbian military in its anti-NATO information warfare campaign."

After confirming the identities of the hackers and ensuring the quality of their intelligence, Swallow and Knesek utilized the informants to assist the FBI in its mission to protect the U.S. information infrastructure during the NATO campaign in Kosovo. These contacts gave them access to the global, underground world of hackers. Knesek and Swallow now had connections. In fact, they had worked undercover as hackers themselves. Using an alias, Swallow had slowly become a known entity to hacker crews. He had status. They trusted him.

When the main NATO operations in Kosovo ended in late 1999, it became clear that the team's work had put the FBI in a position to further infiltrate the hacking community at large. They had found a way in. Neal pushed the FBI and U.S. Department of Justice to authorize them to continue their work, but with a new focus. "Thus, the first official undercover operation designed to penetrate the U.S. hacker community was born," wrote Verton, who revealed the existence of the operation in a 2001 article in *Computerworld* magazine. Until then, the operation had remained secret.

"The FBI has gained a foothold in the hacker underground thanks to an 18-month undercover operation launched during the height of the U.S. military's 1999 bombing campaign in Kosovo," noted Verton. "What started out as a Defense Department operation designed to ferret out pro-Serbian hackers responsible for the April 1999 denial-of-service attacks against U.S. government and NATO Web sites soon led to the first coordinated undercover operation targeting U.S.-based hackers."

In 2000, Swallow moved to further establish his hacker credentials within the community. On more than a dozen occasions he was given authorization to deface government websites and claim credit in order to bump up his status.

"It took about six months to really get them to feel comfortable enough to pass information along," Swallow told *Computerworld* in 2001, after he had left the FBI for the corporate security world. "I had hackers pass stolen credit cards to me and request help in hacks."

The hackers Swallow hung out with on IRC thought he was one of them. Many days, he simply logged on to IRC channels as his alias and watched as other hackers chatted about attacks, new exploits, or crimes they had committed.

ON FEBRUARY 7, the day of the Yahoo! attack, Swallow followed his usual routine and found his way into some of the IRC channels frequented by hackers. The conversation was dominated by discussion about who had hit Yahoo!. According to *The Hacker Diaries*, Swallow had previously encountered me on IRC, describing me as a "loudmouth script-kiddie." That night, Swallow claims, I entered the same channel he was in and began boasting about having pulled off a major hack.

Again, I don't recall engaging in any of my typical boasting that night. I was still in shock about what had happened to Yahoo! earlier in the day. The test of my new attack had worked better than I'd ever imagined. I remember many people claiming responsibility for the attack that night, but I don't recall being one of them.

The next evening, though, any hint of restraint on my part disappeared. Apparently, Swallow sat and watched as I verbally sparred with people who doubted my abilities. I was flush with power and ego that night. Plus, some punk had tried to upstage me by taking down Buy.com.

Soon the challenge was issued: No one could take out CNN. Minutes later, CNN's website ground to a halt and I was back in the channel, looking to receive my due for what I'd done. Swallow took note.

Also taking notes on that session was Michael Lyle, then the chief technology officer at Recourse Technologies Inc., a California security company. Lyle was a self-described computer whiz in his early twenties when the attacks occurred. He had served on the security team at Exodus, a major web-hosting company in California whose clients were targeted in my attacks. (After being contacted by Neal of the FBI, Exodus turned over all of the relevant information contained on its servers. This evidence would prove very useful to the FBI in tracking me down.)

While Swallow moved around online in hacker circles, the FBI's Neal and Knesek were also on the case. The team that had been so effective during the NATO attacks was now fully engaged.

At the same time, Lyle, working independently, was hot on my trail. He began popping up in IRC channels trying to chat with anyone bearing the Mafiaboy handle. Lyle was possibly one of the first people to believe I was responsible for the attacks. Most, including Swallow, initially thought my skills were too rudimentary, so they looked elsewhere.

Lyle eventually went public with his suspicions. In a *Washington Post* article of February 15, he said that "we entered into a number of conversations with Mafiaboy and we saw him asking for suggestions on what sites to attack and after someone would suggest a site, that site would go down."

Lyle's work, while eventually vindicated, was at the time ridiculed in the hacker community. Many thought he had little evidence to support his claims. They also thought he was trying to get press for himself and his company. The online hacker magazine *2600* would later produce a transcript of a conversation between one of its writers and Lyle in which the writer posed online as Mafiaboy. After Lyle spoke with the press and claimed that Mafiaboy was a suspect, the *2600* writer logged on to IRC with that nickname and engaged Lyle in conversation in order to show that "all one needs to do to be considered a suspect is change a nickname on IRC. We had absolutely NO proof that we could provide to make this fictitious person responsible in any way for the attacks."

That conversation, which took place on February 10, five days before the FBI publicly named Mafiaboy as a suspect, would prove to be prescient. The *2600* writer using the Mafiaboy nickname in IRC decided to include a little bit of French in the conversation as a red herring, to make Lyle think he was dealing with a Canadian in Quebec. It was a total coincidence.

In the exchange, Lyle is logged on with the user name icee, and Mafiaboy is the *2600* writer posing as me.

ICEE: From the RUMORS i'm hearing, the only thing keeping you out of jail at the moment is geopolitical issues, and the fact that they don't think you're behind all of the attacks

ICEE: I think the general idea is, they're going to swoop in, get you in custody, and then when you can't talk to anyone else or do anything else, completely fuck you over

ICEE: So I have a couple of different recommendations, depending on what road you want to take

ICEE: 1) get a lawyer, surrender to custody, try to plea bargain

ICEE: or 2) publically [sic] make a statement

ICEE: because if you don't do something now, your ability to talk to the rest of the world is going to be limited

ICEE: if it looks like you didn't know what the fuck you were doing, things can turn out a lot better

ICEE: and I have some information, that i certainly can't say over the phone, that could be of great value to your defense attorneys

MAFIABOY: and whats in it for you

ICEE: What is in it for me?

ICEE: You pick option #1, nothing

ICEE: You pick option #2, I'd like to be the person who leads you forward

ICEE: But that's also up to you

MAFIABOY: and then you write a book

ICEE: I don't want to write a book

ICEE: i want to sell software

As Lyle continued his independent hunt for Mafiaboy, the FBI was ignoring me—even though Swallow had watched as I took down CNN.com. He and his colleagues were inundated with tips and felt it was too early to key in on any one suspect, especially since IRC channels were filled with people claiming they had launched the attacks.

After taking down Dell.com on February 12, I once again logged on to IRC to chat with my fellow TNT members. My mouth was in overdrive that night. I was by then wise enough not to use the Mafiaboy name and had logged on to the #!tnt channel as "anon," meaning anonymous. Freed from the association with Mafiaboy, and inside a private TNT chat room, I naively thought I was safe to let my mouth run free. But my chat session that evening would become a damning piece of evidence against me.

T3: mafiaboy, so who's next after dell

MSHADOW: you know wait till they talk about it on msnbc

SWINGER: ms should be next, and drop the chat server

ANON: t3 tonight I put this computer in the fireplace

SWINGER: heh

MSHADOW: haha

ANON: I aint joking

MSHADOW: why don't you just take out the hd [hard drive] and kill that then put a new one in

ANON: mshadow I don't want to take ANY chances

MSHADOW: really. And talking on IRC is not a chance?

ANON: what can irc prove?

T3: mafia

ANON: uhm fuck it, fuck the fire place, sledge hammer instead

T3: it's spoofed, they can't catch you, I need to get away from you before I get busted for being an accomplice or some shit

ANON: t3 don't give a fuck

MSHADOW: haha

T3: heh

ANON: don't take chances

T3: aren't you going to go out with a bang at least?

ANON: yes

MSHADOW: drop like 10 core routers :\

ANON: no

T3: what are you gonna do

ANON: Microsoft

ANON: Microsoft will be gone for a few weeks

T3: HAHAHAHAHAHAHAHAHAHAHAHAHA

T3: oh man, that's evil

ANON: maybe, I'm thinking something big, maybe www.nasa.gov, or www.whitehouse.gov, maybe I'm just bluffing

T3: I need to get away from you before I get busted for being an accomplice or some shit

ANON: t3 "hit the router"

ANON: the whole router list

ANON: I know what im doing

ANON: yahoo.com

T3: haha

T3: So Mafiaboy, it was really you that hit ALL those ones in the news? Buy.com, etrade, eBay, all that shit?

ANON: you just pin em so hard they cant even redirect

ANON: t3 maybe. Who knows. Would only answer that under ssh2

T3: haha

ANON: I might [encrypt] the hd and sledge hammer and through [sic] it in a lake

T3: they say you're costing them millions

ANON: surprised I didn't get raided yet, t3, they are fools

The log of that chat would eventually be fed to the FBI by several sources. I had managed to escape their scrutiny even after an agent sat by as I took out CNN's website, but this chat session caused law enforcement to refocus their attention on Mafiaboy. Just as I had indicated in the chat, I soon covered my hard drive in magnets to destroy the data, smashed it to bits, and dropped it off a bridge into the water below.

Meanwhile, the FBI was making its own preparations. Agents began searching the internet for clues to my identity and soon found an account in the name of Mafiaboy registered to an ISP in Canada. Data from the Dell attack also pointed to another ISP in Montreal. It started to look as though Mafiaboy was in Canada.

Another piece of the puzzle would later be found by network administrators at UC Santa Barbara. I had used some of their servers in the attacks, and their team had kept the relevant logs. During their own investigations, the administrators also discovered a hacking tool on one of the compromised servers. It had been registered to a familiar name: Mafiaboy. My sloppy hacking habits, in combination with my big mouth, were starting to help the FBI.

The FBI, however, was faced with the reality that I wasn't the only person using the Mafiaboy handle online. Other Mafiaboys had turned up in the United States. So who was the real Mafiaboy? FBI agents debated the issue, but one person had already made up his mind.

"[Charles] Neal was adamant that the real culprit was sitting across the border in the Montreal area," writes Dan Verton in *The Hacker Diaries*. Armed with the evidence of the accounts in Montreal, my chat sessions, and the data from UC Santa Barbara, the FBI was now ready to take its search across the border.

ON FEBRUARY 14, the FBI placed a call to the RCMP and asked for assistance in tracking down a Canadian hacker who went by the name Mafiaboy. The file was soon handed over to a Montreal RCMP officer. Luckily for the Bureau, he had experience in computer crimes. Back in the summer of 1999, he had been brought in to help the FBI when it was investigating the breach of a small ISP in Oregon called Outlawnet. RCMP Corporal Marc Gosselin was now on the case.

On February 15, he executed search warrants at Delphi Supernet and TotalNet in Montreal, the two ISPs that had been linked to a Mafiaboy account and the sell.com attack respectively. He soon discovered email accounts using the name Mafiaboy at TotalNet. As he looked through the information connected to the accounts, something began to seem familiar. He tried to jog his memory by going over some of his older cases. Corporal Gosselin picked up the file for the incident at Outlawnet in Seattle and soon realized what it was about the TotalNet account information that was nagging at him. It was the same telephone number and address he had collected while investigating the Outlawnet incident.

Corporal Gosselin, who declined to be interviewed for this book, later told author Dan Verton that was the moment he believed he had found the real Mafiaboy. The hacker, it seemed, lived in a house on Rue du Golf. The Outlawnet case had gone cold and been relegated to the filing cabinet. But now it appeared to offer the key link that would show that Mafiaboy was in Montreal, and that he had a history of hacking.

In just over a week, my mouth, in conjunction with server logs and recent and past deeds, helped put key evidence in the hands of the RCMP and FBI. Their case was rapidly progressing, and all signs pointed to a large house on a quiet street on the West Island of Montreal.

The timing of the breakthrough was ideal. The same day Corporal Gosselin made the link to the Outlawnet case—February 15—was the day the world would hear about Mafiaboy. The White House and U.S. Department of Justice had made sure of it.

CHAPTER THIRTEEN

Dad, It Was Me

*Federal agents chasing the hackers who brought down a string of
high-profile Web sites are preparing to question several suspects in the
case, sources familiar with the investigation said yesterday.*

*One of those people, "Coolio," is located in the United States,
the sources said.... A second is allegedly a Canadian teen known
online as "mafiaboy."*

*Law enforcement officials and independent cyber-sleuths have been
able to link the online aliases to real names and addresses, and FBI
agents are expected to begin questioning them as early as today.*

*Meanwhile, representatives of some of the biggest high-tech
businesses are scheduled to gather at the White House at 11 A.M.
The companies have agreed to jointly call for a voluntary, industry-
led coalition that will share information on cyber-attacks and how to
respond to them—a step that security experts hailed as critical to
discouraging future attacks ...*

—"FBI Set to Query Hacker Suspects;
Agents Have Linked Names to Aliases,"
The Washington Post, February 15, 2000

At 11 a.m. on February 15, 2000, U.S. president Bill
Clinton convened a White House summit on cybersecurity. In
attendance were executives from America Online, Yahoo!, 3Com,

Cisco Systems, Sun Microsystems, IBM, AT&T, Hewlett Packard, Intel, Microsoft, and other companies. There were also academics, officials from the National Security Agency, and several well-known computer security experts.

The day before, Clinton made history by being the first U.S. president to grant an online interview. He spoke to CNN.com in order to quell fears about online security and send the message that his administration was on the case. "These denial-of-service attacks are obviously very disturbing, and I think there is a way that we can clearly promote security," Clinton said.

The next day he gathered the group of executives, academics, and experts in the Cabinet Room of the White House. The media were invited in to report on some of the proceedings. CNN carried parts of it live.

"We know that we have to keep cyberspace open and free," Clinton said. "We have to make, at the same time, computer networks more secure and resilient, and we have to do more to protect privacy and civil liberties."

February 15 was the day Mafiaboy was officially named as a suspect. In addition to that key piece of information, *The Globe and Mail* reported that the RCMP was now involved in the investigation. Also that day, the *Toronto Sun* revealed that an ISP in Toronto had been served with a warrant. These details combined with the release of the suspects' online aliases and the White House summit to give the impression that serious progress was being made by law enforcement. That was indeed the reality, especially thanks to Corporal Gosselin's efforts in Montreal to confirm my identity.

ABC correspondent Bob Woodruff summarized the FBI's efforts on that evening's newscast, saying, "The search for suspects now involves four foreign companies and all fifty-six FBI field offices." Although he noted also that there was a certain level of impatience among the press and the public, "agents insist the trail has not gone cold, despite the fact that a week after the worst hacker attack in U.S. history, there has not been a single arrest."

People wanted to see those responsible for the attacks brought to justice as soon as possible. The FBI, the U.S. president, RCMP, and other governments and agencies were all doing their part to make it happen.

I, however, was in school when major news was breaking about my case. I had no idea that my alias had been reported in *The Washington Post* and other media outlets that morning, or that it had gone out on all major newswires that day. Unbeknownst to me, Mafiaboy had become the stuff of headlines. Law enforcement had proceeded far enough in their investigation that it now informed the press of its desire to interview "Coolio" and myself. Another hacker, "Nachoman," was also added to the list.

I remained unaware of the news about my attacks until that night, when, sitting on the couch at my friend Brian's house, we flipped through the channels and landed on CNN. I then heard my online alias broadcast for the first time. Although I can't be certain it was the same report I saw, here is what a CNN correspondent reported that night:

> Sources tell CNN a number of hackers who may be tied to the attacks on major Web sites now have the FBI knocking on their doors. Among them, a Midwestern hacker who goes by the screen name "Coolio." He's suspected of defacing a security firm Web site last weekend, using an electronic signature that matches the one used in last week's large-scale attacks. And "Mafiaboy," a Canadian teenager. Investigators say he recently suggested in internet chat rooms he was interested in attacking Web sites.

I felt sick to my stomach as my alias was read out on live TV. They even knew I was Canadian, something that up until now only my friends on IRC knew for sure. Brian sat next to me, oblivious that he was sharing a couch with Mafiaboy. I had been so careful for so long to keep my online identity separate from my offline life. Now Mafiaboy had followed me from the virtual world onto live TV. It was like I had come face to face with my own creation. A CNN reporter was talking to me and tens of thousands of other people about Mafiaboy. It was surreal. I was on CNN! This was trouble. I was in some serious shit.

Brain sat there, unfazed, letting the information pass him by as if it were just any other story. I felt the urge to lean over and tell him, *It's me, bro*. It was suddenly too much for me to handle, too much to keep inside. In the end, I wasn't able to restrain myself. I told Brian I was Mafiaboy.

When he was finally convinced, I felt relieved to know that someone I trusted, someone who knew me as Michael, now understood the other persona I had been hiding for the last few years. That sense of relief was fleeting. Brian was in shock, and also more than a little impressed.

"You did that shit, bro?"

"How did you do that?"

"The FBI is after you!"

"You're on fucking CNN!"

He had questions, but I wasn't in the mood to offer answers. I knew there was a hot-tempered forty-five-year-old Italian somewhere on the West Island of Montreal who needed to be the next to hear what I'd done. Unlike Brian, he wasn't going to be impressed. How the hell was I going to explain this to my dad?

THERE ARE MANY THINGS YOU DISCOVER about your parents as you grow up. Things you often have to learn the hard way. With my father, there were a couple of important rules I had already tested and verified.

Rule Number One: Don't Mess with His Cigars

My father loves his cigars. One of his happiest moments of the day is when he gets home and has a chance to sit outside with a cigar in his mouth. That's his time. You don't bother him when he's smoking, and God forbid you move his cigars or try to sneak one from him. He'll know. Because of his work, my father has bus schedules and routes programmed into his brain. He also has a section devoted to his cigars: the brands he has smoked, where his cigars are in the house, and how many are left. Mess with his cigars and you see the living incarnation of the famed Italian temper.

Rule Number Two: Meals Should Not Be Interrupted

This is a somewhat complicated rule. My father loves good food and ideally loves being able to enjoy it in a calm atmosphere. But unlike a cigar, which can be butted out and saved for later if something is hampering his enjoyment of it, food is best eaten when it's hot and fresh. So, even though you shouldn't bother him when he's eating, it can be a good time to calmly spring something on him. Sometimes even bad news comes second to his desire to enjoy his meal. The key is *sometimes*. It's a risky strategy, but it can pay off.

There are more household rules, and many of them have nothing to do with keeping your distance from my dad. Those of us who know him well know that he's a big teddy bear at heart. He loves his family, cares about the people around him, and will break his back to help them. Call that Rule Number Three. It was why I knew I had to tell him. I needed his help. I was a scared kid in way over my head. Rule Number Three came first to my mind. Then, when thinking about how to tell him, Rule Number Two provided the answer.

The news of the hunt for Mafiaboy had hit on a Tuesday. I waited a few days and thought about how I was going to tell

him. Soon it was the weekend. I couldn't wait any longer.
At one point, the house was empty except for the two of us.
It seemed the perfect time to talk to him, especially when I saw
him sitting in the kitchen eating a panini. A panini is the food
equivalent of a cigar for my father. I realized there was never
going to be a more perfect moment. The sick feeling returned
to my stomach as I shuffled into the kitchen and sat next to my
father at the table. I could smell the panini and see that he was
enjoying it.

"Dad, I have to tell you something," I began.

"Okay. Is something wrong?" he asked.

"I don't know how to explain this, but have you seen what's
going on in the news?"

"What do you mean?"

"The attacks on Yahoo! and CNN, have you seen that on the
news?"

"Yeah, what about it?" He continued eating his panini, more
puzzled than concerned. And perhaps a bit annoyed. *What the hell
are you talking about CNN for? I'm eating a panini!*

"I don't know how to tell you, but I'm the one responsible for
the attacks," I said. He looked up at me, panini held mid-air.

"What are you saying?"

I explained that I was the one who had orchestrated the attacks
that were all over the news. That teenager they were looking for
in Canada? It was me. I was Mafiaboy. I had messed up really bad.
He continued eating his panini. He was calmly taking it in.

"All those times you wondered what I was doing on the
computer for all those hours?" I said. "Well, I guess now you
know."

He looked at me, not saying anything for a few seconds.

"Michael ... tell me, are you joking?"

"No, I'm not."

It was starting to register. With each successive bite of his panini, he took in what I had said. He chewed. He swallowed. He thought some more and took another bite. After a couple more bites, he had digested what I had told him. The panini went down on the table.

"Okay," he began. "On Monday morning we go see a lawyer and explain what you did. We have to prepare for this."

"Dad, I didn't get caught," I said. "Why are we going to see a lawyer?"

In my mind, seeing a lawyer was the same as confessing. I had hoped there was a way to wait this out, to put my faith in the separation between Mafiaboy and me.

"What if you do get caught?" he said. "It's better to be prepared than get caught with your dick in your hand."

EARLY THE NEXT WEEK, my father and I drove to Nuns' Island, an affluent community near Montreal, to meet with a lawyer, someone my father had known for years. I didn't want to see the lawyer. It meant I would have to tell yet another person about Mafiaboy. My secret was slowly becoming other people's property. That too-familiar sick feeling lodged in my stomach. I was being put into situations I wanted no part of, had no choice in. But I was slowly realizing that by my actions I had brought all of this on myself.

As we waited in the conference room for the lawyer, I calmed myself by looking out the window and picking out the buildings I knew off in the distance, back on the island of Montreal. Sitting high up in this building with gigantic windows, I felt set apart from the crush of the city. My stomach relaxed. Then the door burst open and a man flew into the room. He had brown hair, brown eyes, and an average build. I immediately noticed his defined jaw and how white and shiny his teeth were. He had a wide smile, a shark's grin. He moved like a shark, too: gliding with power and precision. This, I thought, was a guy who knew how to take care of business.

"Eh, John, what's happening?" he said, patting my father on the back.

He knew we were there for something serious and urgent, but he was jovial and calm. He seemed ready for anything. He and my father caught up on the latest news with each other. I managed to relax. This lawyer was giving me a good feeling. He was so charismatic that I almost forgot why we were there. My father and he ended their small talk and the man directed his attention to me for a moment. Then he looked over at my dad.

"This is the younger one or the older one?" he asked.

"The younger one," my father answered.

I stood up to shake his hand.

"Yan Romanowski," he said.

"Pleasure to meet you. I'm Michael," I said, wanting to show him I was mature and professional. I wanted to impress him. He shook my hand and quickly turned to my dad.

"You didn't tell me he was better looking than you, John," he said.

We all laughed and then Yan and I took our seats. It occurred to me that he still didn't know why we were here. He seemed to be enjoying the meeting. What would happen once he was let in on my secret?

"So what's the story guys, what can I do for you?" Yan asked.

My dad looked at me and said, "You'd better tell him, because I'm still not exactly sure what you did."

I began to explain the situation. Yan said he had read about the story in the media. I told him every detail that seemed relevant—which sites I had attacked, how I had done so, and that the FBI had announced I was a suspect. By the time I was done explaining, I could tell he was surprised and perhaps even a little impressed.

"*Tabarnac,*" he swore in French. "You are the one responsible for that?"

I nodded.

"Now you can see why we needed to see you," I told him.

Yan looked back at my dad and grinned. "Hey, John, you know how to do that stuff?"

"Are you crazy?" my dad said, almost bursting out in laughter. "I know how to use a fax machine, that's about it."

Yan chuckled and looked back at me.

"I can barely use my email—you must be a genius to know all that stuff," he said.

I was pretty much in the palm of his hand at this point. He had managed to calm me down and keep my father and me laughing. But now it was time to get serious. His face tightened and he straightened up. With just a few motions, he transformed himself into a no-nonsense criminal lawyer. My father and I leaned in to listen.

Yan wanted to know what evidence I had left behind and if I thought I was going to get caught. I explained there were other suspects but that I appeared to be the top one. Because of the size of the attacks and the publicity they got, I figured there would be an extensive team of experts deciphering the logs and searching me out. The conversation had got dead serious and, in my mind, very grim.

"The best thing right now is to stay low key and don't do anything," Yan said.

He paused, looking as if he was thinking about which piece to move next on a chessboard.

"Who knows, maybe they won't find you," he said. "Either way you look at it, they need to make the first move. The best thing to do is prepare for the worst. You can expect if they do find out your identity that they will come for you when you least expect it."

My father and I remained silent as Yan finished his assessment.

"For all we know, they could be monitoring you already, so be very cautious of whom you talk to," he said.

That last sentence hit me in the gut. *Jesus, they could have us bugged!* It made total sense, but it hadn't yet occurred to me that the police could already know my true identity. I began running through the possibilities in my mind. Had they put the word out about looking for me in order to make it seem as though they didn't know my real identity? Maybe they were parked outside? Maybe my bedroom was filled with tiny microphones? Had anyone been following me?

Yan had painted a disturbing picture. All I could do was take his advice and lock down everything I did. No chatting, no hacking, no more people added to the Mafiaboy Secret list.

"The best we can do now is wait," Yan said. "But Michael, I don't want you to worry too much. If they do come for you, I will be there before you can blink."

I swallowed hard and prayed that he was right.

CHAPTER FOURTEEN

Suspicious Minds

THE MAN WAS CLEARLY NERVOUS. He walked in unannounced to the offices of the *Mirror,* a weekly Montreal alternative newspaper, and said he had a story to tell. The man was passed to Philip Preville, the news editor. Preville encouraged the young man to share the story with him. The source looked to be in his late teens or early twenties. He was fidgety and cagey. "It was almost like he was concerned he was being followed," Preville, now a contributing editor at *Toronto Life* magazine, recalled in an interview.

This Mafiaboy thing, the man said, I know about it. I know him. We're related.

Preville's interest was piqued. The day before, February 15, he had read news reports saying that the FBI was after Mafiaboy, a teenage Canadian hacker, in connection with online attacks against U.S. e-commerce giants. Could Mafiaboy be in Montreal? This guy said so, and he seemed freaked out. Maybe there was something truly Mafia about Mafiaboy.

"I thought he was either telling the truth or that he was a really good actor," Preville said. "When you work in alternative media, people come [into the offices with a story] and if they're lying, they brag." It was unusual to have someone come into the office claiming a personal connection to an international story while also acting scared. "There was no sense of brazenness, and that counted for something as I tried to size him up," Preville said. "You usually expect people to come in and brag and not be scared."

Preville listened as the man explained that Mafiaboy was his cousin. He said they had done a bit of hacking together, though the man said he himself wasn't involved in the major attacks. "The guy gave every indication that he had regular contact with Mafiaboy," Preville said.

In the end, Preville decided the story was credible enough to run in the coming week's edition. "Last Wednesday, the *Mirror* received an unexpected visit from a man claiming to be a close relative of Mafiaboy, the internet hacker currently sought by the FBI in connection with the recent shutdowns of high-profile Web sites cnn.com, amazon.com, e-Bay, and others," read the February 24 article, under the headline "On the trail of Mafiaboy." "The man appeared genuinely scared."

"I'm freaked out for Mafiaboy," he was quoted saying. "The police will be knocking on his door soon. It's only a matter of days."

According to the article, the man also wanted to make the point that "a few fingers ought to be pointed at the e-commerce giants for the lax security that made the mischief so easy to carry out.... There's another side to this story that isn't getting told," he said.

The source had made another interesting observation. "Mafiaboy has never paid a cent for internet access in his entire life," he told Preville.

That was very close to the truth. My father paid for our internet access at home, but I also had access to pirated internet accounts. After the FBI phoned in 1999 to offer a warning about hacking activities emanating from our home, my father had temporarily taken away the main internet account, but I always had access to cracked accounts. This person who claimed to know me seemed to be aware of that. Was it just a lucky guess? Or was this guy really a relative? My sense is that only someone close to me and familiar with my activities could know about the pirated accounts.

For Preville, the story ended there. He never heard from the man again, and no one responded to the article. "I felt like it was a bit of a go-nowhere story and didn't know how to follow up from there," he said. "But it was a good story to walk in the door so I did it."

Preville's source turned out to be correct on a few points, the most important one being that I was in Montreal. This was not widely known at the time. In the ensuing years, the article has also gained in credibility for another reason: At some point during the investigation, someone close to me became an informant for either the RCMP or the FBI. It's possible that the nervous man who showed up at the *Mirror* in February 2000 is the same person who worked with law enforcement.

IT WAS ONLY DURING RESEARCH FOR THIS BOOK that I came across the *Mirror* article and began to realize its possible significance. After my arrest, I learned through Yan that the RCMP claimed to have an informant, though we were never told anything about this person. The RCMP and FBI later offered a few tidbits of information about the informant for the 2002 book *The Hacker Diaries*.

"Although the details remain a closely guarded secret, the FBI and the RCMP acknowledge that an informant played an important role in identifying Mafiaboy and letting agents know when he was online," writes author Dan Verton. "There are still questions about who the source might have been and how the source might have verified that Mafiaboy was online. The RCMP and FBI are not talking."

There was also mention of an informant during the court proceedings prior to my sentencing. While on the witness stand, Corporal Marc Gosselin spoke about reviewing "evidence that was provided to me by the FBI and that was provided by a confidential informant ..."

I had known all along that there was another way for law enforcement to nail me for sure, and this weighed heavily on me before my arrest. What if a fellow member of TNT, or someone else who knew that Mafiaboy had launched the attacks, decided to rat me out? What if the FBI already had an informant in TNT?

The FBI's operation to infiltrate the U.S. hacker community had caused Swallow to be in the right place when I bragged about my exploits in IRC and then hit CNN.com. I, of course, had no idea about this at the time, but I had always had suspicions about some of the other hackers on IRC. At the top of the list were T3 and Mshadow, the two members of Core who had been recruited into TNT after their group disbanded. I was often wary of T3 because he asked me a lot of personal questions. Mshadow was also on my radar because he never did any hacking and had a habit of asking me personal questions. He hung out on IRC with the rest of us but didn't engage in battles to take over channels or go after other groups. If anyone was a fed, I thought it would be him.

Suspicion was a necessary virtue among the hackers on IRC. Everyone used handles and various technical measures to try to hide their true identities and real IP addresses. It was an unwritten rule that you don't divulge anything even remotely incriminating to someone you don't know. But T3 and Mshadow had been vouched for and invited into TNT, so I felt I had to accept them on at least a certain level. That's why, despite my suspicions, I engaged with them and Swinger in that incriminating chat when I was online as "Anon."

When I read over that transcript now, I can't help but see how they were egging me on, playing to my ego. I was like a child trying to show off for the older kids at school, trying to prove how tough and smart I was. In reality, it was the dumbest thing I'd ever done online—except for the actual attacks, of course. My desire for credit and status caused me to cast aside my suspicions. Perhaps T3, Swinger, or Mshadow was in fact agent Bill Swallow. I'll never know. Also unclear to this day is how many informants there were. Someone was passing transcripts of IRC chats to the FBI. Was the same person also notifying it when Mafiaboy was online? Was the informant Corporal Gosselin referred to in court the same person mentioned in *The Hacker Diaries*? And what about the source of the *Mirror* article, my supposed relative—how does he fit in?

One similarity between the *Mirror* article and the description of the informant in *The Hacker Diaries* is that both refer to someone close to me. That person knew where to find me online. I do have a lot of cousins, which is how the man who spoke to the *Mirror* described himself, but none of them ever did any computer work with me. I have a brother and a stepbrother who both know a bit about computers, but, again, neither of them did hacking with me.

Then there's my friend who worked as the administrator of an IRC server run out of a large U.S. university. He was my informant. Not long after the attacks, he got in touch with me online and said the FBI was contacting IRC administrators. Agents were after chat logs from specific channels, and my contact said they were also planning to track certain people. Watch your ass, he told me. His warning was another reason I decided to dispose of my hard drive. Of course, he also could have been the person tipping off the FBI about my online activities. It's hard to know who to trust when you're dealing with aliases and adopted identities.

If it seems like I'm going in circles—well, that's exactly how I feel. I have suspicions to this day but haven't been able to confirm them. The man who spoke to the *Mirror* appears to have been smart enough to offer credible details and then tack on untrue elements—such as the claim that he was my cousin, which to me seems implausible but was perhaps meant to make him appear more plausible, or to lead authorities astray. And, of course, the RCMP and FBI aren't talking about their informant. Especially not to me.

Back in 2000, I had no idea that the people around me would be eager to help the FBI or RCMP, or willing to take their story to the press. Looking back, all of these elements seem better suited to a spy novel than the life of a fifteen-year-old kid hacking away in suburbia. As I went about my life, Bill Swallow was lurking online in many of the same channels as I was, an informant was tipping off law enforcement as to my activities and identity, and a supposed family member felt the need to tell a local paper that I was in Montreal.

For the FBI and RCMP, this abundance of information was good news. For them, things were about to get even better.

CHAPTER FIFTEEN

Wiretapped

ON FEBRUARY 18, Jill Knesek of the FBI stepped off a plane in Montreal. Corporal Gosselin's work establishing my identity had moved the case to its next phase. Knesek would now be the Montreal-based liaison between the FBI and RCMP. If Mafiaboy was in Montreal, the case would belong to the RCMP. But that didn't stop the FBI from wanting to be a part of every aspect of the investigation: Even if the culprit was in Canada, the U.S. Department of Justice considered the case to be an American one. Whoever was responsible had compromised servers at American universities to attack major U.S. companies. There was no way the FBI was going to back off and let the Mounties take control—or all the credit.

"The number of requests for information coming from Washington was mind boggling, and the RCMP had grown increasingly distrustful of the officials in Washington," writes Dan Verton in *The Hacker Diaries.* "They became reluctant to share a lot of information with them. After all, the case now fell clearly within Canadian jurisdiction."

Sending Knesek to Montreal was a way for the FBI to cultivate a strong working relationship with the Mounties and keep U.S. authorities in the loop. Knesek and Corporal Gosselin managed to move past the bureaucratic and jurisdictional jockeying and work together. On the same day Knesek arrived in

Montreal, the RCMP installed digital-number recorders on our house in Île Bizard. Unlike a wiretap, a DNR records only the numbers dialled from a particular line. They could tell who was calling whom but couldn't hear what was being said. Nevertheless, the DNR was useful because it would reveal the dial-up numbers used to connect to the internet. This could help law enforcement learn if multiple internet accounts were being used inside the house.

That was in fact the case. But the question remained, which ones were being used by Mafiaboy? The RCMP knew that, besides me, my father and stepmother, as well as my older brother and two stepsiblings, lived in the house. But they still didn't know who was doing what online, or which of the kids was Mafiaboy.

That changed on February 25. The RCMP and FBI obtained a court order for a wiretap on our house. They would now know who was saying what to whom and could also collect data on exactly what was being done online. It went live on February 27. Yan's warning about wiretaps had come to fruition only days after our meeting.

For my part, I was focused on trying to behave at home and at school as if nothing had changed. I went about my usual activities—including causing trouble at school—but I had a creeping sense of the inevitability of my arrest. Yan had said the authorities would come when I least expected it. The question was, what evidence would they have? I often thought of my old hard drive at the bottom of the river. Would that bit of foresight be enough to keep me out of jail?

Although I didn't attack any more high-profile sites, I continued to hang out on IRC and converse with my fellow TNT members. I also worked to try to learn more about hacking and programming. Worst of all, I kept logging on to U.S. university networks where I had previously obtained accounts. I was still breaking the law. In retrospect, my behaviour was reckless and stupid. I should have reduced my online activities to nothing more than basic email and web surfing, but I was hooked. I couldn't stay off IRC and didn't want to disappear from TNT. I also wanted to keep learning and advancing my skills. As the FBI's Swallow would later explain in a 2001 article in *Information Security* magazine, this kind of behaviour is typical of hackers: "A lot of [hackers], I think, just get addicted. Having been there myself for a year, I can tell you it's a very addictive kind of behavior. There's a real power of being able to break into a computer system anywhere in the world."

The same addiction and hubris that caused me to launch repeated attacks against e-commerce giants continued to influence my online activities. This only ensured the RCMP would have plenty of evidence against me. In the end, the forty-three days of wiretaps would yield 7.6 gigabytes of data from the online activities in my house.

Agents downloaded daily data logs and pored over them to establish exactly which member of the house was Mafiaboy. (At first they thought it was Lorenzo.) The RCMP also listened in on phone conversations, most of which were fairly mundane. Officers were treated to conversations between Lorenzo and his friends, my stepbrother and his girlfriend, and me and my friends. One RCMP summary of a conversation between my friend Brian and me in early March reflects two typical teenagers chatting on the phone:

> [Michael Calce] talks about basketball. Michael talks about
> Brian boxing his dad. Brian talks about the relationship
> with his parents. Michael talks about his work, his
> paycheque. Michael puts his money away to go buy
> clothes in the U.S. Talks about the Boston Bruins. There is

a basketball game on TV. Michael mentions he is sick.
They talk about girls.

Fascinating stuff. But there was incriminating material
peppered in with the boring daily conversations. My situation
was fodder for a lot of phone calls. Our entire family was
fixated on the press attention because each new story seemed
to float a theory about who I was, whether I was guilty, and
why I had launched the attacks. One article in particular
caught our attention. Author Naomi Klein penned an open
letter to Mafiaboy in the February 23 edition of the magazine
The Nation:

> As I write this, the Federal Bureau of Investigation and the
> Royal Canadian Mounted Police are closing in on your
> position. Maybe you are already behind bars, imprisoned
> for crimes against Yahoo.... Like so many who have
> secretly cheered your exploits (if indeed they are your
> exploits), I can see through the nihilistic pranksterism to
> another kind of Mafiaboy. My mythic Mafiaboy isn't a
> vandal but an anticorporate freedom fighter for the
> e-commerce age.

As Klein notes in her column, others in the press viewed me as a
"vandal," a "spitballer," and as being "antisocial." She continued,

> The old-school hackers, their straggly ponytails freshly
> blow-dried, have been meeting with Bill Clinton and
> Janet Reno to help them nail you. These hackers claim
> they are motivated by love. They love technology—they
> just want it to work properly. But Mafiaboy, I believe you
> were committing an act of love too: not for the integrity
> of a particular line of code, but for the Internet in general,
> as it could have been.

I remember reading Klein's column and wishing that had been the case. My brother also thought it was a great piece of writing and began telling people about it. On March 7 he called Sergio, a friend who ran a computer company and knew I was Mafiaboy. Lorenzo knew about Yan's warning about wiretaps, but he wasn't alone in ignoring it. The RCMP recorded the conversation.

Lorenzo: Uh … this … this person … what's her name … Naomi … Naomi something.
Sergio: Okay.
Lorenzo: She wrote a whole article about Mafiaboy.
Sergio: You're not serious.
Lorenzo: A whole like … but I'm talking like an article uh … like praising him, you know.…
Lorenzo: … You're going to find this very interesting actually uh … I've never read a story like this.
Sergio: Yeah?
Lorenzo: She's very … I don't know what the paper must be … one of those papers they write a lot of strong [articles] … you know what I mean like … the way she wrote it … it was as if … she was basically telling all the e-commerce, "Fuck you." That's what she was saying.

Sergio soon asked if Klein was "a good looking girl" because he thought maybe she was interested in me. They had a good laugh about it, but that story was passed around among my family and friends. I told my father about it that same day, noting that she was making me look good. Klein had eloquently made an argument in favour of what I had done, but my true motivations had been far less admirable.

That day, March 7, saw a flurry of calls from our house. At around noon I discovered that someone had registered mafiaboy.com and put up a website about me. I browsed the site, which gathered articles about my case, and soon phoned my brother's cellphone. I was fixated on the press coverage and mafiaboy.com. It was easy to get caught up in all the events taking place outside our house. As a result, I too ignored Yan's warning that our phones might be tapped.

Me: You will not believe this.
Lorenzo: What?
Me: You know Mafiaboy.com.
Lorenzo: Yeah?
Me: Someone registered it.
Lorenzo: Yeah.
Me: And there's a whole page about me.
Lorenzo: No way.
Me: And there's all kinds of …
Lorenzo: Are you serious?
Me: Yeah, dude.

Not long after that, I called my father, either on his cellphone or at work, I can't remember now, to tell him about the site.

Me: Some interesting stuff I'm finding.
Dad: Yeah, what?
Me: You know Mafiaboy.com?
Dad: Yeah?
Me: It's registered.
Dad: Is it?
Me: The whole page is about me.
Dad: What about it?
Me: I don't know it says everything … there's all kinds of stuff …

Dad: Is it good though? They got you?
Me: They got me? They know shit.

The owner of Mafiaboy.com didn't know who I was, but thanks to conversations like that, the RCMP sure did. Their wiretaps proved that I was Mafiaboy.

Along with the constant media speculation about my identity, my attacks attracted attention because they caused governments and companies to announce new initiatives aimed at combating hacking. The Canadian Defence department created a team of twenty scientists and computer specialists to fight off hackers.

"Although the Defence Research Establishment computer team's main function is to protect Canadian Forces information systems, it will also likely provide the research and development role for a planned national co-ordination centre to fight off hacker attacks on key Canadian computer systems," said a February 28 Canadian Press report on the initiative.

Earlier in the month, Attorney General Janet Reno appeared before the U.S. Congress to argue in favour of a proposal to spend $2 billion in 2001 to help safeguard the United States' critical information infrastructure. I couldn't believe the chain reaction that had been set off by my actions.

Back in the press, rumours abounded. Various publications managed to unearth so-called hackers and experts who claimed to know who I was. *Maclean's* magazine published a lengthy interview with Rachelle Magliolo, a woman who went by the handle VetesGirl and claimed she was a veteran hacker. She said she knew exactly who I was, and that I had attacked her in the past. She said I lived "within fifteen minutes of Toronto" and was sixteen or seventeen years old. Wrong. But she and I did have a history.

I first came to know VetesGirl when I was hanging out in #warezIWC, the channel I found when looking for warez. I was a newbie at the time, begging Drakus to teach me how to hack. VetesGirl and I were both new to the channel and we became friends. I moved on when the group disbanded after Drakus's disappearance. After going solo for a while, I was invited to join Alpha. I'm sure she would see it differently, but it seemed to me that she became resentful. I had moved beyond her into a more elite crew. Things between us deteriorated from there, with the two of us battling verbally on IRC.

"I've known Mafiaboy online for a couple of years," she told *Maclean's* in 2000. "He's a malicious little kid, a typical packet kiddie."

By the time the article came out, we had long since moved past verbal sparring. I had hacked her website, self-evident.com, and battled with her on other occasions. The truth is, most of us in TNT considered her to be a bit of a joke. But if it sounds like I was the only one stirring things up between us, that wasn't the case. At one point she wrote a scanning program that could be used to check computers to see if they were vulnerable to certain exploits. It's common for someone to give some shout-outs to other hackers they know when releasing a program. In hers she listed people with handles such as "RainMakir," "Eosyn," and "rajak," among others. But below those props she included this line:

Fuck You: @efnet mafiaboy, metaray, tabi, matrix, meta, _sk, antionline …

She portrayed herself to the press as being above the usual IRC poor behaviour, but it was a lie. She was in there mixing it up with everyone else. Yet in the aftermath of me being named a suspect, anyone like her who claimed to know important details about me was handed a big microphone and never challenged about their claims. Everyone said I was a trash talker, which was true, but they were the ones feeding bullshit to major media outlets to make themselves look good.

There were people like Naomi Klein who saw me as a subversive anti-capitalist hero, and others like Magliolo who sought to save the reputation of "real" hackers by insisting I was nothing more than a packet-wielding punk. Article after article in February and March 2000 purported to reveal the truth about Mafiaboy, but none of them came close.

ROB CURRIE, the head of the RCMP Computer Investigative Support Unit, may have felt that he was one of the few people in the world beginning to see the truth about me. Currie was the man charged with monitoring internet activity inside our house. He occasionally watched in real-time as I went online. Soon, however, the flood of data was overwhelming. That was because, after much nagging by the kids of the household, my father relented and installed high-speed internet access in March. This, according to *The Hacker Diaries,* caused Currie to set up a computer lab in the basement of his home to deal with the onslaught of information.

The data were coming in at a furious pace. Evidence against me was rapidly accumulating, but the RCMP was still unsure if they had everything they needed. They had logged me using stolen accounts on various university networks, and they had also watched as I went on IRC and gathered more stolen accounts.

In addition to my usual online activity, I was often online with my friends David and Patrick. Both now knew I was Mafiaboy. The RCMP recorded our activities as we occasionally launched attacks against each other and chatted on IRC. On March 26, I was on the phone with Patrick as we both logged on to IRC. We talked about a potential attack against a certain channel and,

according to an RCMP summary of the conversation, Patrick
began talking about the attacks against Yahoo! and the other
websites:

> Michael says that he is going on IRC and that Patrick is
> there as Monkey man ... Patrick asks Michael when he is
> going to do that shit again. Michael gets upset and tells
> him never to talk about this again ...

The pressure was starting to get to me. Only a couple of weeks
before, I was marvelling at the press coverage and enjoying Naomi
Klein's article about me. That changed on March 8 when Coolio,
one of the American hackers named as a suspect in the attacks, was
arrested. In real life he was Dennis F. Moran, a seventeen-year-old
high school dropout. "Moran surrendered without incident and
was charged as an adult with two counts of unauthorized access
to a computer system," reported CNN.com. "Each charge carries
up to fifteen years in prison."

Fifteen years for each count! This got to me. Coolio was
arrested for gaining access to and defacing DARE.com, a government anti-drug website. Now he was facing decades in jail.
(According to CNN, he had defaced the site by covering it with
pro-drug messages and the image of Donald Duck with a
hypodermic syringe stuck in his arm.)

Moran's crimes were far less serious than mine. I wondered
what would happen to me if and when I was caught. I kept up a
brave face, telling people that it would be much harder to catch
me because I wasn't in the United States, and that authorities
there hadn't even contacted me yet.

The truth is, Moran's arrest scared me, especially because it
appeared the FBI knew he hadn't taken part in the attacks against
Yahoo! and the other websites. That meant there would be even

more attention focused on me. I called my dad on March 8 to tell him about the arrest. The RCMP summary of the call was matter of fact: "Michael tells his dad about the arrest of Coolio the hacker. Michael says that Coolio is no longer the suspect in last month [sic] attacks on the major sites."

Lorenzo also phoned my friend Mike to tell him that I would get less time in prison because I was younger than Coolio. Less than two charges of fifteen years? That was hardly a comfort. Maybe I'd only be up for five or ten years in jail. It was tough to think about. Yet I still couldn't keep myself offline. I *had* to be on the computer, on IRC, accessing all of those hacked accounts. Even the threat of years in jail didn't end my obsession. The RCMP just sat back and watched as I continued to break the law.

The wiretaps had initially been authorized for sixty days, but the RCMP decided to suspend the interceptions sooner than expected. Beginning in late March, the RCMP had begun paying close attention to a specific series of phone calls involving my father. He was talking with people about a business associate who was causing him problems on a joint venture. My father had put money into a bus operation in Ottawa. He soon realized that the man who ran the operation had put a lien against the business and was conspiring to cut my father out of the deal. My father was going to lose more than a million dollars, and this was beginning to wear on him. When speaking with friends, he used language that struck the RCMP as potentially dangerous.

I've read the transcripts of the conversations and can see how the RCMP may have been concerned, because they had no idea what my father was like. When he gets upset he vents verbally but doesn't do anything physical. He speculated with a couple of friends about finding some way to get after the guy. One such phone conversation occurred on March 27. At one point, his friend said, "Break a few legs I can understand."

"I gotta see some boys," my father said. "I'll fix it up."

Soon after that, they talked about an upcoming First Communion. Then they had this exchange:

John: We don't owe him nothing so it's easy to get [the lien] off. It's just he's inventing shit and he's gonna ... he's gonna prolong ... I'll get it off but, you know, how long will it take.

Friend: Personally, give him a good beating or something ... that will tell him to take things off.

John: Eh?

Friend: That's probably just as good.

John: Yeah.

Friend: I think so.

John: You do?

Friend: ... You can get him so fucking scared that he [takes the lien] off. That's probably a route.

John: Yeah?

Friend: ... scare the shit out of him, fuck. So?

John: Oh! He'll shit his pants for sure. But then you open [sic] a can of worms then you know?

My father and his friend went back and forth with the fantasy, but no action was taken, and no plans made to take any. Subsequent media reports would say that my father had hired a hit man to kill his business associate. This never happened. My dad was just playing out fantasies over the phone. We're not mobsters. Still, the RCMP began to think, as Knesek later told author Dan Verton, that I didn't "pull the name Mafiaboy out of the air."

A couple of weeks later, on April 14, my father spoke with a man about getting some repairs done on his vehicle. He mentioned the situation with his business associate and how it would result in expensive lawyer fees. "John says he wants to get this court case over with so he can breathe," noted the RCMP transcript. Then the transcript quotes this exchange (which I partly translated from French):

John: In case your friends are ready, give me a call.
Man: Okay.
John: I'd like to do a fuckin' number on that fucker.
Man: Exactly.

Then they go back to discussing the repairs on my dad's vehicle. It was a recurring pattern: some heavy talk followed by the subject being dropped completely. While I realize this probably sounds Mafia-esque to a lot of people, remember that, in the end, the charge against my father was dropped. The RCMP had some suggestive transcripts, but even they and the prosecutor realized there was nothing to them. In my opinion, the RCMP saw an opportunity to gain leverage by arresting both me and my father on the same night. That was likely seen as a good reason for cutting short the wiretapping, especially considering the RCMP now knew that I was Mafiaboy. They had me on tape taking credit for the attacks and had recorded me committing other breaches of computer system security. So, on April 14, the decision was made to raid our house on Rue du Golf.

Mafiaboy and his Mafiadad were both going down.

CHAPTER SIXTEEN

"Open the Door or We'll Break It Down"

AT ABOUT 3 A.M. ON APRIL 15, my father and stepmother were in bed asleep as a group of cars and vans filled with officers from the RCMP and other law enforcement agencies pulled up in front of the house. My brother, Lorenzo, was out for the night, and I was sleeping over at a friend's. As I sat on a couch several blocks away watching *Goodfellas,* an RCMP officer took out a cellphone and dialled my home phone number.

The ringing woke up my father. He grabbed the receiver and checked the clock, wondering why someone was calling the house so late. The voice at the other end said he was with the RCMP and that my father should "open the door or we're going to break it down."

My father's first thought was, "Go ahead, break it down." He was still half-asleep and didn't know what was going on. He put on a robe and went downstairs to open the door. Instantly, officers swarmed the house. The officer who seemed to be in charge took my father into the kitchen and told him he was under arrest. He started pushing and grabbing my father, so my father pushed him back. Meanwhile, my stepmother, having followed my father downstairs, was frozen with fear. The officer, Corporal Gosselin, was a big guy, and she was scared he was going

163

to hurt my father. Finally, a more senior officer stepped in and told Corporal Gosselin to take it easy.

"Look where he lives," he told Corporal Gosselin.

My father thought the officer was suggesting that this wasn't the home of some crazy crook that they needed to manhandle. The senior officer was diplomatic and seemed smart; my father thought that maybe they planned it to look that way—good cop, bad cop.

"Look, don't touch him," said the officer, and everyone calmed down.

My father asked what they were arresting him for and was told it was because he had threatened someone. He didn't know what they were talking about.

During the first few minutes of the raid, it was clear to my father that the police were surprised. They had thought I was at home. My dad told them where I was, as I wasn't trying to hide. Meanwhile, the police continued their search, asking if we had any guns on the premises. My father told them no, we didn't deal with that kind of stuff.

According to my father, there were twenty-five or thirty officers in our house by now—RCMP, FBI, local police. There was a parade of different uniforms, and some of the officers were in civilian clothes. They walked throughout the house, grabbing the computers and carrying them out. They told my dad to call me to inform me that the police were coming to pick me up. A few officers left to bring me back home, while others asked my father if he knew what I'd done.

"I knew he had been doing stuff with the internet, but I'm not familiar with that stuff," my father recalls telling them.

They pressured him to tell them everything he knew, saying it would make things easier on me once I was in custody. "Talk to us before we … get your son," one officer told him.

Sitting in his bathrobe at three in the morning and watching police swarm all over his house, my father had no intention of saying anything.

After a few more questions, the officers saw they weren't going to get anywhere, so they told my father that it was time to take him in. My father called Yan, our lawyer, and then asked to go to his room and change into some clothes.

"We need somebody to go with you," an officer said.

There was no way my father was going to let someone watch him change, so he told the officer to either let him get dressed by himself or to just take him in his robe. The officers, having by this time checked the house and found nothing dangerous, let him get changed by himself. As he got dressed, my father wondered if he knew the whole story of what I had done. The police's actions just didn't seem to make sense. He began to worry about what he didn't know.

My father returned downstairs, and officers tried to handcuff him for the trip downtown to the Montreal police station, but the cuffs didn't fit, since my dad's hands and wrists are huge. The police were starting to get frustrated.

"Look, I won't do anything drastic," he told them.

They agreed to leave off the cuffs. They led him out to a car and drove off—he wouldn't be around when I was brought back to the house.

At the police station my father was put in a holding cell with three other men. Just by looking at them, he could tell they all were high on something, so he asked to be moved to an empty cell. The police refused, so my dad started shaking the bars and calling out for them to move him, which they did. About twenty minutes later, Yan arrived.

Later in the morning, my father went before a judge via video-conference and posted $1000 bail to secure his release. He had to agree not to come within a certain distance of the man he supposedly tried to harm.

"I went home on Saturday morning and knew that Yan had things under control," my father told me when we sat down later to talk about the night of the raid. "I was comfortable that you were in his hands."

AFTER BEING PICKED UP and then processed at RCMP headquarters, I spent the weekend at the Cité Des Prairies detention centre. I was finally released on Monday morning. Thanks to the bail conditions set out by the judge, I was prevented from using computers and the internet, had a curfew, and was also prevented from seeing my three best friends, Brian, David, and Patrick, even though none of them had been involved in the attacks.

At the time, I assumed separating us was a way of punishing me while I awaited trial. I had expected the other conditions, but this was a surprise. It was also the most difficult one to obey. I was used to seeing them every day. Now I had to cut off all contact. (I later saw wiretap transcripts that showed me going online to chat with them, as well as us discussing hacking and the attacks. I guess this was why the RCMP wanted to keep us separated, even though it seemed clear to me that none of my friends had been involved in the attacks.)

When my arrest was announced that Wednesday, I stayed home from school for a few days because of the ensuing media frenzy. Although I wasn't exactly a devoted student, school was part of my daily life, my routine. I spent the next few days trapped inside my house with no internet, no contact with my best friends, and the media stationed out front. I felt like a prisoner.

By the following week, the media trucks had moved off our street and I was allowed to return to class. Everyone at school now knew that I was Mafiaboy. People pointed at me and whispered when I walked down the halls. Some students, often kids I didn't even know, came up to me and asked questions.

"How did you do it?"

"Why did you do it?"

"Did you know what you were doing?"

It was frustrating to constantly be asked the same questions over and over. I was known as a loudmouth and troublemaker at school, but I didn't want this kind of attention. I didn't do the attacks to earn a reputation at school or with the press. Now millions of people knew about Mafiaboy. My secret identity had been compromised. My connection to the world of TNT and IRC had been severed. It was a nightmare.

I will admit, however, that there was one unexpected benefit: girls. I often had girlfriends, but now I was the resident bad boy. I appeared dangerous, and a lot of girls liked that. Given the seriousness of my situation, though, it was of small comfort.

The rest of my school experience only got worse. I walked the hallways a marked man. Cut off from my best friends, I let my already slipping grades hit rock bottom. The school required every student to wear a uniform, but I began letting my appearance slide. I'd leave my shirt untucked or find various ways to rebel against the uniform, among other rules. Each violation earned me a blue slip. The slips began piling up, bringing me close to disciplinary action, but I didn't pay any attention to that mounting problem. I was more concerned about what the FBI and RCMP had in store for me.

Meanwhile, my dad and I made regular trips to meet with Yan and discuss how I wanted to proceed. I had two options: pleaded guilty or not guilty. The decision would be influenced by the quality of the evidence the prosecution had against me. But we hadn't received any information from the prosecution yet.

While we waited for copies of the evidence to arrive, Yan deflected inquiries from the press. He had advised me not to say anything, but the requests were constant. Every major North American news outlet contacted Yan at some point, all of them begging for an exclusive. He made a few comments immediately after my arrest but soon stopped talking. Yan had never dealt with press on that scale before, but he knew enough not to get wrapped up in all the attention. In typical Yan fashion, he used it to lighten the mood. "They even want to know what kind of toothbrush you use!" he told me one day.

The requests from the press began to taper off as the school year ended. I was still prohibited from going online and couldn't see my friends, but the summer release from school was a welcome change. The only problem was that we still didn't know what evidence had been gathered against me. Yan told me to expect further charges. We knew the house had been bugged, and I often tried to recall potentially incriminating conversations. What had the RCMP heard? I knew they must have logged me going in and out of various university networks in the weeks after the attacks, but this struck me as unrelated to the case. I wasn't worried about that.

I spent the summer waiting for the information that would dictate my future. Late in the summer, I got a taste of the level of scrutiny I was under when I was sent to a detention centre for two days for coming into contact with the friends I was forbidden to see.

It had already been the lousiest summer of my life, but the worst was yet to come.

CHAPTER SEVENTEEN

Eighteen Days in Hell

A teenager accused of crippling CNN's Web site will face 64 new charges, a Crown prosecutor said Thursday.

The 15-year-old boy, who called himself Mafiaboy on the Internet, was scheduled to appear in court Thursday afternoon to face the additional charges, said prosecutor Louis Miville-Deschenes.

Most of the 64 charges to be laid deal with hacking into computers, Miville-Deschenes said in an interview outside court.

The rest involve denial of service [attacks] against other major Internet sites, including Amazon, e-Bay and Dell.com.

The allegations are very serious, Miville-Deschenes said.

"General deterrence is a major issue in a case like this because you want to show everyone it's a serious matter," he said. "The mischief that was caused involved serious damages for all of the victims."

—"Teen accused of crippling CNN's Web site faces more charges: Crown," Canadian Press, August 3, 2000

On August 3 I was hit with sixty-four new charges in connection with attacks I launched before and after hitting CNN.com. We still hadn't received copies of the evidence against me, but the Crown prosecutor apparently had enough to go after me for the websites I had knocked offline and the many computers I had compromised while under surveillance. They wanted to hit me with as many charges as possible in order to scare me, and to send the message that Mafiaboy and anyone like him would face a harsh penalty if caught.

I again pleaded not guilty and did my best not to be too freaked out. I knew I'd be back in school in about a month, and that was another source of worry for me. I wanted no part of my senior year. I was in grade eleven, the final year in Quebec's high school system. (Students then head to CEGEP—the Quebec equivalent of community college—for two years before going on to university.) Senior year of high school is supposed to be one of the best times of your life, but I had no interest in school and had no intention of attending a CEGEP. I wasn't excited about graduating and didn't care about any of my classes. I had tried to improve things by asking to be transferred back to Lindsay Place, my old school. I thought it would be better for me there since everyone at Riverdale knew I was Mafiaboy. The principal of Lindsay Place had agreed to let me return, but Riverdale had to approve the transfer, which it denied. I had no choice but to return to Riverdale in September.

I was sixteen years old and facing close to seventy charges that could put me in a juvenile detention centre for a maximum of two years. I was still prohibited from seeing my three best friends and going online, and I had a court-imposed curfew. Now I had to attend a school I wanted nothing to do with. My life was in shambles.

I began accumulating blue slips pretty much from the first day back at school. I soon had enough for a one-day in-school suspension, the typical punishment. That meant I went to school in the morning and spent the entire day with other troublemakers in a special classroom. We were allowed to leave the room only to go to the bathroom. Still, it was nothing compared with two years in a detention centre.

The school sent weekly reports to my dad to keep him abreast of my progress, or lack thereof. He cracked down on me and told me my behaviour had to improve. The weekly reports frequently detailed me talking back to teachers, disrupting class, skipping school, and earning poor marks. I felt under watch at all times but did manage to make some improvement with my attendance and conduct in class. But I soon reverted to my old habits.

"We began to see some reversals in Michael's behaviour this week," the vice-principal's letter reported to my father for the period of November 28 to December 1. "He had two very positive weeks (Nov. 15–26) and we were hoping for continued improvement. He remained in all of his classes save two. I did receive a report from a teacher of him walking out of his English class ... and he was asked to leave his French class on November 30 for poor behaviour and rudeness."

The letter reported that I had left my shirt untucked and worn a jacket inside, which constituted uniform infractions, behaviour that once again earned me an in-school suspension on December 1, but the letter included the positive note that "teachers still speak of the progress he is making ... Michael has shown a willingness to make an effort and co-operate with staff."

The letter was sent on December 4 and is notable for a glaring omission. By the time the vice-principal sent it, I was already back in jail.

ON DECEMBER 1 I was in the suspension room serving my penalty when a teacher told me to go to the vice-principal's office. I walked in and was shocked to find Corporal Marc Gosselin sitting there. He grinned at me and stood up.

"What's this about?" I asked the vice-principal.

"You've breached your bail conditions," he told me.

"You're going to be coming with us today," said Corporal Gosselin.

One of my bail conditions stipulated that I not get in trouble at school. I was unaware that even something as mundane (to me) as an in-school suspension was a breach of my bail conditions, particularly because I had had in-school suspensions before. Corporal Gosselin was smiling because he was there to arrest me. I asked to call my lawyer. Yan said there was nothing he could do right away and that I had to go with Corporal Gosselin. I was in shock. They were taking me into custody because of an untucked shirt?

Corporal Gosselin appeared to take great pleasure in the fact that I was caught off guard. "You're going to be arrested and transported to court," he told me. He put me in handcuffs and marched me toward the school's entrance. In my opinion, there was no reason for handcuffs, and we could have easily taken a path that wouldn't have required me to be frogmarched in front of students and teachers. But I don't think Corporal Gosselin was interested in helping me save face. I felt he wanted to embarrass me, to hold me up to ridicule in front of as many people as possible. He may have seen this as another way to apply pressure and make me pleaded guilty.

Students and teachers fell silent as I walked through the building in cuffs. I felt like a caged animal at a zoo, a curiosity. I could imagine them thinking, "What did he do now? Launch another attack?" No, I had acted out in class and left my shirt untucked. Now I was in handcuffs. I was definitely embarrassed. More than that, I was enraged.

I was escorted into the backseat of a waiting RCMP vehicle and we made our way to the courthouse downtown. In contrast to the relative silence of my previous ride with Corporal

Gosselin, now he used our time together to work on me. I think he was hoping I would crack and give myself up. But I saw it as a personal battle: me against him. Who would get their way?

He kept at me the entire journey. He said that the RCMP had me nailed. He smilingly told me I had just made a big mistake. He was going to make sure I spent time in custody now. No mercy. "You should pleaded guilty, do the judge a favour," he said. He obviously didn't understand how my thought process worked. I was resolved not to let myself be influenced by him. If I was to pleaded guilty, it would be my own decision—not because he had slapped me in cuffs and paraded me in front of students and teachers. That only served to make me resent the cops even more. Like most teenagers, I didn't like being told what to do or to be embarrassed in front of my peers. Corporal Gosselin was pushing the right buttons to get me upset. But rather than making me want to give in, it made me search for ways to make it hard on him. Payback. That meant not cooperating.

Since December 1 was a Friday, I spent the weekend and following Monday in jail. On Tuesday, December 5, I went in front of a judge to try to regain my freedom. The prosecutor told the court that I had received multiple suspensions at school and was failing every class except gym. (The media reports all made note of my failings at school.)

The judge took the breach of my conditions seriously. She denied me bail, and I was immediately sent back to a juvenile detention centre. I was beside myself with anger. I was mad at myself for having let something as stupid as blue slips put me in this situation, but I was also angry with the RCMP and the judge. My father, too, was upset by what was happening. Our family had never been in trouble with the law before; this was new and confusing. It seemed that the RCMP and prosecutor had the upper hand. I didn't fully appreciate how easy I had made it for them by continuing my downward spiral at school. Now my actions had brought me back to jail.

I WAS SENT TO THE NORTHVIEW UNIT of the Shawbridge Youth Centre. From the outside, it looked like a normal school. It was a low building with a playground. Unlike Cité Des Prairies, there were no high fences or razor wire around the perimeter. As a result, kids were frequently AWOL from Northview. I never tried to run, but I thought endlessly about how I could get out of there.

Rather than being a place for rehabilitation, Northview was, albeit unwittingly, a crime school for kids. There was a set routine for each day of the week: You got up at a certain time, ate a certain time, and did specific activities and took classes at a certain time. Some days you were allowed time in the gym or swimming pool. There were movie nights. That was all to be expected. But I soon observed how little time the staff spent working with all of these troubled kids. We were left to interact with one another with little or no guidance.

What does a large group of troubled, law-breaking kids do when left to their own devices? They make new connections, share stories of crimes, and pass along tips for burglarizing, selling drugs, or other dubious activities. A kid could go into Northview for something relatively minor and come out with a whole new set of criminal skills. The state of affairs at Northview brought to mind Johnny Depp's line in the film *Blow* about his time in prison: "I went in with a bachelor's of marijuana and came out with a doctorate in cocaine." Northview offered master classes in juvenile delinquency.

Aside from time spent with other kids, I passed the days locked inside a small cell with disgusting custard-yellow walls. My family visits on Sundays were the highlight of each week. In between visits, I focused on my upcoming hearing, where it would be decided if I could once again be released on bail. A hearing in youth court on December 8 had been unsuccessful. Then, on December 13, my trial date was set for March 5. In the meantime, I was still refused bail.

Yan came up with a strategy to get me released, and so he scheduled another hearing at the Palais de Justice. I was going to adult court. Since my breach was misconduct at school, Yan and I decided our new approach would be for me to work full-time. The idea was that I would have an easier time staying out of trouble if working. In order to get out of jail, I had to drop out of school.

In early 2000, I had started working part-time at Le Biftek, a steakhouse. Yan now thought it best if I left school and focused solely on work. We hoped this would persuade a judge to release me from Northview. I knew, though, that the judge might not agree and that I'd have to remain at Northview until my trial in March. I prayed to God that wouldn't happen. Even though I was able to play basketball and go swimming, I had no illusions about Northview being anything but a jail. That point was driven home when we were in class. While I had always been the biggest disruption in classes at Riverdale, I marvelled at my fellow delinquent students. When a bunch of them were put together in a classroom, all hell broke loose. Nobody cared about learning, and no one respected the teachers. Most of their time was spent just trying to keep us kids in line. I often enjoyed the commotion around me, but my attention was almost completely focused on my December 19 hearing in Superior Court.

I had never been to adult court. I wondered if this meant I would be held with adult criminals—the real deal. I had a recurring vision of pulling out a cigarette and having a big guy with tattoos come over and snatch it out of my hand. I had a lot of reservations, but adult court seemed our only option to get me back out on bail. December 18 was by far my worst night at Northview. I was sleepless and consumed with fear. What if I had to stay here until March? I wasn't sure I could deal with that. Christmas at Northview. The idea made me shudder.

By the time morning came, I was already dressed and eager to move. I was led outside, where I was surprised to find a police wagon. My last trip to court from Cité Des Prairies had been in a somewhat everyday van, though there was a glass shield behind the driver. Was this change because of my hearing in adult court?

The back doors of the wagon opened, and I looked in to see two men sitting inside. I panicked. I was being thrown in with adult criminals. Would one of them be the burly, tattooed cigarette snatcher of my recurring vision? Fortunately, neither one said anything to me. We each had our own problems to worry about. Despite the silence, I had a sense of what one of the men was in there for because he stunk of booze. I guessed he'd had a rough night in a drunk tank somewhere.

The van turned into an underground entrance for the courthouse, where I was separated from the others. Two officers took me in an elevator up to a cell. Wait here, they said. I was relieved to have a cell to myself. I had dodged the cigarette snatcher.

Officers eventually came and took me to a room next to the courtroom where I could see and hear what was going on inside. It was like a private box for convicts. I thought about the times I had watched a Canadiens hockey game from similar seats and hoped I'd soon be able to enjoy that privilege again.

Scanning the faces in the courtroom, I began to worry. Yan was nowhere to be seen. I wondered if I had been brought to the right place. I became even more worried when I heard what was being said in the courtroom. The judge was deciding whether to grant the release of a man accused of stabbing his wife or girlfriend (I don't remember which) about five times. He said that he had blacked out and woke up with a knife in his hand. Now here he was, asking to be set free. The lawyers argued, the judged asked questions.

Jesus, I thought, I really am in adult court.

I expected this guy to get sent back to a cell, but he was released on bail. I couldn't believe it. Then I realized that my chances were pretty good if a guy accused of stabbing somebody could get released that easily.

Then it was my turn. When I walked into the courtroom, I saw that a lot of the seats were filled. Reporters had heard about the hearing. Notepads in their hands, they stared at me as I entered. But I still couldn't see Yan. The judge was rummaging through papers and didn't even look up at me. Now I was really anxious. Where the hell was Yan? Finally, my father entered the courtroom. I began to calm down. I was in the right place. I would get my hearing.

Yan came in with the prosecutor. They had been dressed in business suits for my youth court appearances. Now both of them wore black robes. The judge read my file and asked Yan to explain what the hearing was about. I told myself that everything would be fine. But the judge who had seen fit to release the guy accused of stabbing someone began arguing with Yan about taking me out of school. Children belong in school, he said. He looked at me and sternly noted that I shouldn't be breaking school rules.

I'm screwed, was the first thought that came to mind. *Christmas in Northview,* the second.

Yan explained that the case had brought a huge amount of media attention onto me, my family, and the teachers and other students at my school.

The judge focused on me. If I was let out on bail, I would be put on a very short leash, he said. My conditions would be more severe, and I would be immediately sent to jail if I breached any of them.

It was as if he were Moses coming down from the mountaintop with bail conditions instead of the Ten Commandments. I nodded at everything he said. I felt we were close to securing my release. Maybe I would spend Christmas with my family after all.

In the end, the judge agreed that I could be out on bail as long as I worked full-time at the restaurant and obeyed every bail condition to the letter. I felt a rush of relief. I didn't have to go back to Northview. No more crime school for me.

WORKING FULL-TIME turned out to be the best thing for me. Although I now value education, school wasn't the best place for me then. This was partly because of the environment there, and partly because of my own behaviour.

I had landed the job at Le Biftek because my stepmother was a banquet booker at the restaurant. Before my arrest, it had been a great source of pocket money for me. Although I was never one for homework or paying attention in class, I always took my job seriously. I felt I was learning how to be responsible, and I never got into trouble at the restaurant.

"Mr. Calce is both organized and punctual," read a November 2001 letter from the restaurant's general manager prepared for my lawyer and the court. "He is a very motivated individual with high aspirations for himself. He displays responsibility and dedication, and I recommend him for any future endeavors he may have." In truth, I felt like a completely different person at work than I did at school, more like myself.

Thanks to my hard work and full-time hours, I was given a promotion at Le Biftek. I went from bussing tables to kitchen prep, where my job consisted of helping prepare appetizers and some of the ingredients for the main courses. This meant I earned the right to wear a white kitchen overcoat. I loved pulling that coat on every day. It said I was part of the team. Aside from basketball, TNT was

the only team where I ever really felt a sense of belonging. I had
lots of friends at school but never had the feeling that I was a part
of the school community. (This was, of course, partly because of
how I behaved.) At the restaurant, everything was different. I loved
wearing the kitchen uniform, whereas I had always chafed at
wearing a uniform in school.

I enjoyed my work and loved being in the kitchen with the
other staff. The employees knew me and that I was Mafiaboy,
yet no one bothered me about it. We were there to work. Some
would ask a question or two about my case when we were
outside having a cigarette break, but nothing more than that.
There wasn't any gossiping or whispering behind my back.
My coworkers respected my privacy and treated me as an equal.

I fell into my routine and didn't breach any more bail conditions. Eventually, the documents of the evidence against me
started arriving at Yan's office. He asked me to come in to review
them and explain some of the technical information. At first it
was just a few documents. Then Yan's office began filling up.
There were recordings of the wiretaps, transcripts, server logs ...
the mountain of paper kept growing.

After weeks of reading, Yan called my father and me in to offer
his take on the case. He was convinced that the prosecution would
have a hard time proving it was me sitting behind the computer
orchestrating the attacks. He believed that a lot of the evidence was
circumstantial—and if the police couldn't directly link me to the
attacks with hard evidence, there was a good chance I wouldn't be
convicted. One thing that could work for or against us was the
technical nature of the case. No Canadian judge or prosecutor had
ever before heard a case like this. The prosecution would need to
find a way to make sense of the reams of server logs and data. How
would they clearly explain a denial-of-service attack to a judge?
That would be a challenge. Of course, we would also have to find

ways of showing the flaws and gaps in their evidence. There was nothing simple about this case.

Yan felt strongly that I would have a good chance at trial. Still, the decision was mine to make: I could take my chances and prepare for a long, difficult trial. Or I could pleaded guilty and begin the process of restitution. The RCMP's treatment of me and my father had been difficult for our family, but I was resolved not to let it influence my decision. My old Mafiaboy arrogance kept telling me: Don't give an inch. Don't be swayed by their tactics.

Then, during our discussions, Yan received a letter from the prosecution stating that it would be more lenient toward me if I agreed to pleaded guilty. It was clear that the prosecution and RCMP badly wanted to wrap things up. They hoped to save the time and expense of a trial and be able to show the world that they had brought Mafiaboy to justice.

I have to admit that a part of me was still focused on sticking it to the RCMP. I wanted to stand up to them for the way they had treated my father, and for the time Corporal Gosselin had paraded me in handcuffs in front of my schoolmates. I also felt as though I would lose any remaining online credibility I might still have if I caved in. I had always prided myself on never backing down from an online or real-life fight. This was the biggest battle I had ever faced. Could I live with myself if I simply pleaded guilty? I admit, pride and ego had a strong influence on my decision. The brash loudmouth Mafiaboy was still a part of me.

Another factor in my decision was the trial itself. I would have to continue to be under bail conditions, and spend many days in court. The press would be after me every day. I was already reaching my breaking point thanks to regular court appearances, my time at Northview, being separated from three of my best friends and, of course, having to stay off the internet.

I took time to make my decision, consulting with Yan and my father. They were prepared to fight if that was what I wanted. But by this time, nearly a year after the attacks, I had gained more perspective on my actions. I saw the consequences of the attacks and began to realize and accept that I had caused serious damage. I still hated the idea of giving in to the RCMP, but it became clear that I would have to stand up and take responsibility for my actions.

I asked my father to set a meeting with Yan.

"I'm pleading guilty," I told Yan and my dad. "Let's make a deal."

I believed this meant the media scrutiny, pressure from the RCMP, and bail conditions would soon end. I knew I would serve some time in a detention facility or group home, but then it would be over. I'd have my life back.

I had no idea that even though I was pleading guilty, I was yet to experience the worst of the media attention, and that my biggest court trials were ahead of me still.

CHAPTER EIGHTEEN

Guilty

The National Infrastructure Protection Center and the
Federal Bureau of Investigation (FBI) announced today that on
January 18, 2001, the ... male, known on the Internet as Mafiaboy,
appeared before the Montreal Youth Court in Canada and pleaded
guilty to 56 counts. These counts include mischief to property in excess
of $5000 against Internet sites including CNN.com, Yahoo.com, and
EBay.com, in relation to the February 2000 Distributed Denial of
Service (DDoS) attacks. In each of these instances, the DDoS attacks
prevented the victim sites from offering their web services on the
Internet to legitimate users. The other counts relate to unauthorized
access to several other Internet sites, including U.S. universities.
This investigation was worked jointly with the Royal Canadian
Mounted Police (RCMP), and illustrates the benefits of the long
and productive partnership between the FBI and the RCMP in
investigating computer crime matters.
—FBI PRESS RELEASE, JANUARY 18, 2001

ON JANUARY 18, 2001, the prosecution informed the judge that
I intended to pleaded guilty to fifty-six of the sixty-six charges
laid against me. After a lot of back and forth between Yan and the
prosecution, the attacks and intrusions I would admit to had been
agreed on. These included the DDoS attacks against CNN.com,
Yahoo!, Amazon.com, eBay.com, Dell.com, and some of the

networks at academic institutions I had compromised. I did not pleaded guilty to the attacks against Outlawnet in Oregon. That was ancient history as far as I was concerned. It had no connection to Rivolta.

The press knew I would be in court on the eighteenth, but they were largely unaware that I planned to pleaded guilty. Rumours about me 'fessing up had been floated in the press in the previous months, but this was the real deal. I was going to stand up, admit to my crimes, and face sentencing.

I saw this as a first step toward returning to a normal life. Then I arrived at court and saw that the media presence was greater than ever before. The camera crews—it seemed like there were fifteen or twenty of them—jostled for position to film me entering the courthouse. They did it again when I exited the building after changing my plea. Yan, my father, and I were harassed to give comment. I found it even more unnerving than when the press had showed up unexpectedly at my school all those months before. That had been a surprise, but the number of reporters was dwarfed by those at my proceedings. It seemed they had also become more aggressive. I was now unquestionably guilty; perhaps they felt no need to restrain themselves. I was a crook. We fought our way to my father's car, and I sat in the backseat taking in the scene from behind the tinted windows.

My case now moved to the sentencing phase. To determine my sentence, the court ordered an evaluation by a social worker from the provincial Young Offenders Services. His name was Hanny Chung. Even before I met him, I worried what a government employee would have to say about me.

> Michael Calce is a 16 year, 7 month old youth of Italian
> descent. He measures approximately 5'7" in height and
> about 125 pounds in weight. Michael has brown eyes and

dark brown hair. He also wears a thin moustache and
beard. Michael presented as a clean-cut and well-groomed
youth. He dresses in today's teenage style clothing and
seems quite confident of his own appearance. He also
impressed the undersigned as a sociable youth who
possesses a sense of humour.

This was Hanny Chung's first impression of me, noted in his
eighteen-page report. Chung was a short, skinny man. He was
somewhat friendly but seemed concerned with maintaining a
sense of professional detachment. I was equally cautious of him.
To me, he was on the other team. He worked for the government
and had been assigned to me by the court. I was predisposed not
to trust him, and this likely had an influence on our interactions.
I was never rude or disrespectful to him; I knew enough not to
want to be seen as difficult or insubordinate. But I also had
no intention of opening up to Chung.

I had several meetings with him, and he told me his evaluation
would be a key factor in my sentencing. Chung also met or had
phone conversations with my father, brother, stepmother, and
mother. He received reports about me from Riverdale High
School and my previous school, Lindsay Place, and spoke with
Corporal Gosselin and the coordinator of the Northview Unit at
Shawbridge.

I took our meetings very seriously and did my best to answer
all of his questions, though many of them struck me as strange.
It was clear from the start that he knew very little about the
internet and therefore the nature of my crimes. When he first
asked me to describe what I had done, I responded by trying to
test him. I rattled off a stream of internet networking terms to see
if any of them registered. He seemed to have no idea what I was
talking about. As far as I was concerned, that made it pointless to

try to explain the nature of my crimes. He couldn't understand what I had done. I didn't intend this to be rude, but he took it as arrogance on my part. It wasn't a good start.

Chung asked me why I had committed the crimes, if I understood that what I was doing was wrong, and how I felt about the damage I had caused. Because of his lack of technical expertise, I never felt comfortable with him. I also didn't see how an interview protocol that was often used for violent young offenders could be applied to me. I answered his questions but did so reluctantly. In truth, I wasn't helping my case.

One point I tried to emphasize was that, even though I had caused serious damage, I could have inflicted even more harm. I wanted him to see that I did have some restraint, a sense of right and wrong. I told him that I could have knocked out a lot of the big internet routers on the East Coast if I had wanted to. Big mistake. Chung saw this as bragging. I should have chosen my words more carefully and not mentioned shutting other things down. Or just played the part that was expected of me by acting scared and overwhelmed. I could have handled myself better with Chung, but a part of me wasn't willing to open up or behave as if I was at his mercy. This would come back to bite me.

Chung had already seen RCMP reports noting that I had bragged online about my attacks. Now he felt I was doing it again. "Michael downplayed his involvement in the offence by claiming that he has the capability to paralyze all of the east coast computer systems but did not do so," Chung wrote in his report. "He boasted having the ability to obtain personal information on any customer from credit card companies."

I had told him about how easy it would have been for me to steal personal information and credit card numbers in an attempt to show him that I had acted without criminal intent. But this attempt at demonstrating my sense of restraint failed miserably.

Chung saw me as the braggart of the RCMP reports. His report echoed a lot of what these reports had said about me. Maybe they had been right all along, but at the time I wasn't able to see it or acknowledge it.

I will give Chung credit for seeing through a lie I kept trying to foist on him. I knew the big question on everyone's mind was why I had done the attacks. Was I out to punish the giants of e-commerce? Did I want to become famous? There were a lot of theories. Only I knew the truth: I launched the first attack as a way to test out my new networks and DDoS tool in preparation for Rivolta. Then, after hitting Yahoo!, I became swept up in a haze of ego and hubris. I couldn't imagine explaining to a social worker or judge that I attacked the first site in order to prepare myself for a series of larger assaults against rival hacker crews. I'd look like even more of a delinquent. So I decided to say I was running tests to see the level of security at the websites I attacked. I tried to play myself off as a white hat. Chung wasn't buying it. More importantly, he saw that I wasn't willing to tell the truth about why I had launched the attacks. This was a major strike against me. I felt the lie was a risk I had to take in order to help my sentencing.

I wasn't happy with the way he portrayed me in his final report, but even more painful was the fact that he laid bare some of the issues between my parents. In his summary of an interview with my mother, he wrote that she thought my father's house was a "free for all" because "there was no supervision at all ... the father would allow the two sons to do anything so they would prefer to live with him. He thus, would not have to pay her child support."

Chung noted that my parents "do not have any regular dialogue between themselves. The subject of their children is communicated through their individual lawyers."

Because of my actions, there was now a public record of the difficulties spawned by my parents' divorce. I hated that. I believed that family business should stay within the family. It's not for public consumption. Yet here was a court-ordered report about how we lived.

The final part of my evaluation came in the form of the Jesness Inventory. Chung described it as a "socio-criminological assessment tool used to identify attitude and perceptions that a youth holds in relation to self, others and certain social situations." I sat and answered verbally true or false to 155 statements, including "I'm smarter than most people I know." I was given only a couple of seconds to offer my answer because the point was to capture my initial reaction. This wasn't a problem, as the questionnaire was laughably simple. It was the kind of questionnaire that only someone with sociopathic tendencies or a really twisted mind could show poorly on. In the end, my answers showed that I was not "delinquency-oriented." I was found to possess "a healthy value-system" and be "inclined to adhere to rules and/or limits imposed" on me.

According to the assessment, "[Michael] is capable of differentiating between appropriate and inappropriate behaviour. He trusts people, however, Michael is naïve to a degree and can be too trusting of others at times … he remains susceptible to the influence of others. Michael is a happy individual who feels others generally understand him."

Overall, the Jesness Inventory seemed to confirm that I was a good kid who had done something awful. It also appeared to suggest that I had a good set of values and understood rules and proper behaviour. But something about the results seemed to bother Chung and the colleague who had prepared the evaluation. Chung wrote in his report that, "In his endeavor to possibly present a favourable impression of himself, he may not have been forthright in all his responses in this testing." He offered no further explanation.

Even though there was no evidence to support this suggestion, Chung had pretty much accused me of lying on a true-or-false questionnaire. I was outraged when I saw that sentence in his report. It also seemed to confirm to me that Chung had never been on my side. I did well on the questionnaire so he undercut the results by suggesting that I was lying. His report and subsequent court testimony offered no details to support this suggestion, which was false.

In the end, Chung recommended that I be sentenced to six months in custody, stay on probation until I turned eighteen, make a charitable donation to the Crime Victims Assistance Centre, do a "significant amount" of community service, be prohibited from visiting the websites I had broken into, and attend school or work full-time.

His report had stated clearly several times that I accepted responsibility for my crimes, but Chung felt there was "some likelihood of recidivism." That's why he decided to recommend custody even though, in his own words, it's "not recommended to youth who commit a first property offence." I felt I was getting special treatment because of the high profile of the crimes. Chung had also stated that my attacks had caused US$1.7 billion in damages. He simply plucked the figure from a press report. Even Corporal Gosselin would later disavow that figure when he testified. Yet, as it would turn out, it was a factor in Chung's recommendations.

Chung's report was filed on February 19, 2001. My sentencing proceedings were set for April but then delayed until June. With the RCMP, prosecutor, and now a youth worker all lined up against me, it seemed inevitable that I would be spending time in custody as part of my sentence. Thankfully, Chung didn't recommend I serve my sentence in a place like Northview. It was small charity, but I had to take what I could get.

CHAPTER NINETEEN

My Day in Court

THE FIRST THING I NOTICED was his robe.

Judge Gilles Ouellet entered the courtroom in an elegant black robe that appeared to be made of fine silk. The effect was regal, which was, of course, the point. I stared at him, trying to read his thoughts and demeanour. My fate was in his hands.

Right away, I was troubled by one thing. It wasn't anything the judge said or did. It was something he had no control over. Judge Ouellet was by my guess in his sixties. I couldn't help but wonder how a sixty-year-old man could oversee a hacking trial. He likely had more experience with a record player than with computers. I was convinced that my online exploits couldn't be comprehended by any layperson. Of course, I now know better. I shuddered at the thought of what was to come. It was now mid-June 2001 and my sentencing proceedings were just getting underway. I'd soon know my punishment.

Before court, I had told Yan my concerns about the technical nature of the evidence. He understood and asked me to take notes and suggest questions during testimony. Yan wasn't a technical guy; it was up to me to act as our expert. I was to help Yan poke holes in witness testimony. Since I wasn't going to testify, this would be my major role during the hearings. Right away, I realized I was in a tough situation.

191

The prosecution brought in an expert witness to testify about the technical nature of my crimes. His name was Allan Paller and one look at his résumé filled me with dread. He had degrees in computer science and engineering from Cornell and MIT and was the director of research for the SANS Institute, an organization that offers high-level training in information security. On top of all that, President Clinton had named him as one of the original members of the National Infrastructure Advisory Council. I knew he was likely brought in to shred my claim about trying to run security tests.

The prosecutor asked Paller about his work and academic background. Paller listed off his degrees and the fact that he had been working with computers for more than three decades. He explained that SANS "provides education to about ten thousand people a year in how to protect computers from security breaches."

Well, I thought, I'm screwed.

Paller soon began pulling apart the claim that I was conducting security tests. One of his key points was that you don't run a test on somebody else's system without their permission. He also noted that since a denial-of-service attack is usually aimed at the part of a website that is accessible to the public, it wouldn't be an effective way to test the security level of a company's firewall, the application used to keep out unwanted intrusions. He also explained how a DoS attack worked. I thought he was doing well. Then Paller said something that sent me reaching for my notepad.

The prosecutor asked him, "How can these major sites that were attacked protect themselves?"

Paller responded. "Okay. We've had meeting after meeting on this and we can find no method that a large organization can use that will protect themselves from a denial-of-service attack, or a small organization can use. And the reason is that they use the standard, they come in the standard door and you have to leave the door open so people can, so regular customers can come in. As long as denial of service comes through the door and pretends to be a regular customer, they can, there is no defence ..."

His answer was, in my opinion, completely wrong. There *are* ways to defend against a DoS attack. People on IRC fought them off all the time. My attacks had been extremely powerful, but there are defences. I had seen attacks fail over and over again. I couldn't understand why this guy wasn't talking about packet filters, relays, grids, and other defences against DoS attacks. He made it sound like a person in Australia connected via a dial-up modem could easily launch a DoS attack and take out Yahoo!. I furiously took notes and told Yan to ask this guy about filters and relays.

At one point, Paller appeared to contradict himself. He was asked if a website could block an attack "at their source." Paller replied that "you could if you knew what the source is." My attacks had come from multiple sources, but a good network administrator could start blocking multiple sources once he or she saw where the traffic was coming from. Paller made it sound as if this were impossible. It didn't make any sense to me.

He was later asked about the origins of DoS attacks and how they're used. This again elicited a surprising response. I would have expected him to talk as an expert witness, but he began his reply by saying his information came from "interviews that I've gotten second-hand, so this, I'm going to give you second-hand information." I suddenly didn't feel so intimidated by him. He was an executive at an organization that trains security professionals, yet he didn't seem to understand the hacker community.

He continued, "My understanding is that these denial-of-service attack tools grew up because different groups of hackers didn't like what others were saying about them. And if I didn't like, if one group didn't like what another group was saying, then the second group could flood out the clubhouse. Think of it as a network-based clubhouse."

"Like street gangs?" asked the prosecutor.

"Like street gangs …" said Paller.

I realized that equating me to a street gang thug was likely not going to help my case. I felt Paller was failing as an expert, so I passed notes to Yan on inaccuracies he could capitalize on during the cross-examination. But Paller was an effective witness for the prosecution in other ways, such as when he was asked about my many intrusions into university networks. The prosecutor asked why it was dangerous for me to break into computers even when I didn't cause any specific damage.

"The reality is that it's very much like a person with a highly communicable disease … who has broken into my home and he's walking around my home…." he said. "But since I don't have a clue what he touched, I have the choice of either destroying the entire house or figuring out that he only walked in the kitchen maybe and just destroying the kitchen."

As for my claim of testing security in order to help make things safer, Paller said that "every one of these attacks make us all a little less safe because it paints a picture, it shows a road map of what is possible to people who might want to do it. So I think exactly the opposite is true." If anything, Paller testified, I was making the internet less secure by running my so-called tests.

By the time Yan was ready to begin his cross-examination, I had about three pages of notes for him. Yan began by challenging Paller on his assertion that there is no way to defeat a DoS attack. He also asked him about rerouting and filters. Paller said that rerouting traffic could help fight off an attack, but he also said it wasn't useful. The reason, according to him, was that rerouting was too expensive for companies to do.

He compared rerouting traffic to having a setup of multiple bridges. If an attack knocked out a couple of bridges, traffic could flow onto one of the other bridges. So, yes, he said, this was in fact a way of fighting off an attack. But, Paller said, companies don't use rerouting because "it's way too much money. That's an enormous amount of money.... You don't plan your life because there is somebody out there who is going to do a denial-of-service attack. You just can't. The cost would be huge."

This, I thought, showed that Paller was wrong earlier when he had said a DoS attack couldn't be defended against. The truth was that companies didn't want to spend the money to do it. Paller's statement now didn't lessen my crimes, but it did, to me at least, show that he hadn't been completely accurate in his previous testimony. Yan was brilliant in using my notes to poke holes in Paller's testimony.

Paller had said there was no way I could have been running security tests. He believed I was absolutely out to cause damage. Yet once again Yan managed to get Paller to weaken his first statement. When asked about the nature of testing, he said, "You don't know what anything will do until you do it, I'll buy that"—meaning that it's not always possible to predict that a test will do damage. This was a useful comment in terms of my intention when launching the attacks.

Paller didn't crumble on the stand, but he seemed to have inflicted less damage than I expected he would. He finished his testimony with an answer to a question from the judge that seemed to lay some blame at the feet of large computer companies: "The reason that the computer is not protected," he said, "is that when it is delivered to me, from Microsoft or from Sun

[Microsystems] or from IBM ... it comes with many of the doors and windows left open.... So we believe, SANS believes, that the vendors are going to have to take a much more active responsibility to deliver systems with most of its windows closed."

Paller also noted that, since my attacks in February 2000, "forty-five million new computers have been connected to the internet and many of those are vulnerable to these kinds of takeovers for use in denial-of-service attacks." It was a rather scary conclusion to his testimony, yet one I couldn't help but agree with.

Corporal Marc Gosselin was the next to testify. He walked the prosecutor through the details of my attacks and the subsequent intrusions that the RCMP recorded using their wiretaps. He emphasized that I knew I was breaking the law because the DoS application that Sinkhole and I had developed came with a warning that using the program on a public network was illegal. (This was Sinkhole's way of protecting himself.)

The prosecutor asked Corporal Gosselin about the estimated damage of my attacks, and that mysterious figure of US$1.7 billion was brought up. Corporal Gosselin explained that the figure was projected "by a private firm in the States." He said the RCMP had eventually asked the FBI to gather estimates from all of the companies and universities that had been hit. According to Corporal Gosselin, many of them declined to do so, as they didn't want to draw attention to their losses. Yan rose to object that the claims of damages were hearsay because none of the companies were willing to testify in court.

This was a key moment for me. If the court allowed exaggerated claims of damages to be entered into evidence, it could have a serious impact on my sentencing. As it ended up, Corporal Gosselin did me a favour by knocking down the $1.7 billion figure. Although he followed that by saying I had boasted about my exploits while in chat rooms: "Whether it was on the phone, conversation, or in the chat rooms, he talked in a way that made it very clear that he was very proud of being Mafiaboy, that he was proud that the police did not catch him yet, that the FBI could not catch him. So he was bragging about the events."

Corporal Gosselin agreed with Paller that I was not trying to conduct security tests. He cited wiretap transcripts where I say, "I have shown the entire world that some of the best hackers come from Canada." Once again, my stupid mouth had caught me up.

Corporal Gosselin made a point of noting that "the skill level of Mr. Calce, to my opinion, was not good enough to be able to cover all the tracks he would have wanted to cover."

An accusation of me being a loudmouth script kiddie was inevitable. Yan began his cross-examination by delving into whether it was guaranteed that I would have seen the warning on the DoS program. He also questioned whether a DoS attack can be defeated.

Surprisingly, the prosecutor seemed to do me a favour by following up with questions that made Corporal Gosselin explain how I hadn't stolen information or programs from any companies or universities. He also noted that I hadn't acted for any financial gain, though Corporal Gosselin did say I had spoken about getting a job as a security consultant in the future.

I left the courthouse that first day feeling somewhat positive. There was no doubt that I had done the attacks, but I had pleaded guilty to them. Yan had pointed out the contradictions in Paller's testimony, and Corporal Gosselin could have done worse to me. I was also pleasantly surprised by the lack of press in the courtroom that day. There were only a couple of wire service reports of the testimony, which mainly focused on Paller and Corporal

Gosselin refuting my claim that I had been trying to run security tests. By the end of the day, I felt as though the attention on me was beginning to die down.

COURT RECONVENED ON JUNE 19 with Hanny Chung on the stand. I knew his testimony would be a major factor in my sentencing. Chung's report from February had made it clear that he would be less than charitable toward me.

The prosecutor took Chung through his report, focusing on my claims of performing security tests. Chung batted this away, saying I was unwilling to "grasp the notion" that what I did "was wrong." He noted that I had spoken about moving to Italy to work in security because of how insecure Italian websites were. This was then misinterpreted by the press as me saying I wanted to flee the country and start hacking in Italy.

Chung made note of my reluctance to talk about computers ("He told me these are complicated terms you may not understand") and my "bragging." Chung said that the evidence "demonstrates that he realized that the FBI were after him, and he was very proud they were not able to catch him." He spoke about the inadequate supervision at my father's house, and how I lacked remorse for my crimes. I was waiting to hear him talk about my supposed lying on the Jesness Inventory, but Chung wouldn't offer details. He instead said a colleague had administered the questionnaire and that, therefore, "I don't want to get into details." I hoped Yan would press him on this; I hated being accused of lying on a silly true-or-false questionnaire.

Chung admitted that I had said I would not attack any more sites, but he felt I lacked the appropriate "moral reasoning" to understand what I had done. "Michael does not have the other behavioural problem [sic] like anger management, abuse and all that, but he does have to work on his moral reasoning," Chung said.

It's frustrating to sit in a courtroom and hear a stranger speak about you in such a definitive way. It was his job to evaluate young offenders, and he had been doing it for a long time, but I often felt as though he was talking about Mafiaboy the media creation rather than Michael the sixteen-year-old kid.

There was a brief recess before Yan's cross-examination of Chung. Yan asked me what my thoughts were of Chung's testimony so far. I told Yan that Chung misunderstood me, and that I couldn't relate to him. I felt as though he put a dark twist on whatever I told him. But Yan had learned that Chung had left university without finishing his psychology degree. He had analyzed me and yet he didn't have the educational background that I would have expected.

Yan began his cross-examination by asking Chung to detail his academic background. He focused on why Chung hadn't finished university, why he had left and never returned. Chung said that he pursued a diploma in social work after dropping out of university because that was his area of interest. Yan continued to focus on Chung's seeming lack of expertise.

Chung said, "I think the diploma is important; I mean, it's also important, and learning ..."

"Why, to give you credibility?" Yan asked.

I remember thinking that it was a bit of a low blow on Yan's part to suggest that Chung lacked credibility as a result of failing to complete university, but I was short on sympathy for the man.

Yan moved on from Chung's educational background to his computer expertise. Chung admitted he wasn't a computer expert but a general user. Yan walked him through his lack of expertise, then moved on to the issue of damages, getting Chung to admit that the fanciful $1.7 billion figure cited in his report had been pulled from a press report, not evidence. He also pointed out that Chung had taken behaviour reports from my former schools and not followed up with the people who had written them in order to delve deeper. I thought Yan was doing a masterful job.

One of the biggest factors in my sentencing would be Chung's claim that I lacked remorse. Yan drilled down.

"Give me what would have been remorse for you," Yan said.

"Well, he, again, you know, let me refer back to … He did not take full responsibility of what he did was wrong," Chung said. "He admitted, well, he pleaded guilty, okay?"

"Isn't that taking full responsibility?" Yan asked.

"Yes, he did, legally speaking. But morally speaking, okay, he is trying to explain that, you know, why he was doing something good … he was doing something good to the society, to the companies …"

Chung continued by saying I was trying to offer my security services to companies and that's why I had done the attacks. Of course, this wasn't accurate. I had told him I was trying to test the security of the websites I had attacked, but I didn't say I was trying to offer my services to them. This opened the door for Yan, who then asked him, "To your knowledge, did he, at any time … [take] any steps to contact any of these companies to offer his services?"

"No," Chung said, "I don't know. I have no knowledge."

For the first time, I was actually enjoying being in court. I thought Chung had demonstrated that he didn't have a good grasp of my case. I knew Chung's report would still hold sway with the judge, but Yan was doing an excellent job. He also injected a little humour into the proceedings when he asked Chung why he wanted me to explain how I had hacked into computer systems.

"What information precisely were you looking for?" Yan asked.

"Well, I wanted him to, I wanted to demonstrate or …"

"I hope you didn't want him to demonstrate," cracked Yan.

I enjoyed a silent chuckle. Yan had Chung tripping over himself. Near the end of Chung's testimony, which lasted the rest of the day, Yan asked about the Jesness Inventory. Chung's report noted that I was "not delinquency oriented," but in his testimony he dismissed that and said that I had the capacity to reoffend. Yan pointed out that a person has the capacity to do a lot of things, but that it was a question of intent.

"Did he tell you that his intention one day was to intrude in other computers?" Yan asked.

"No, he did not tell me that," said Chung.

Yan asked about the interpretation of the Jesness Inventory and the conclusion that I possess "a healthy value system." He wanted to know what that meant.

"You are getting into the details of the interpretation which I am not ready to interpret," Chung answered.

"Because you signed this report, sir," Yan said.

"Yes."

"So, normally, if you sign a report, I presume you are in a position to explain the report that you have signed," Yan said.

Not surprisingly, the prosecutor objected. The judge had Chung clarify that he included the work of his colleague who had administered the questionnaire, even though this wasn't noted in his report.

Soon after, Chung's testimony concluded. I felt we had had a good day, but then I had to run the media gauntlet to get to my father's car. Later that day, the media reports came streaming out, all of them noting that Chung had said I lacked remorse and could reoffend. I could only be thankful that the judge wouldn't base my sentence on newspaper articles.

After Chung's testimony, Yan decided to commission our own psychological evaluation. A criminologist came to my house and conducted an interview. I was weary of being repeatedly analyzed but felt better knowing she wasn't employed by the government. The questions she asked seemed more relevant than those on the Jesness Inventory, and I was able to offer more comprehensive answers.

Her report was sent to the judge and to the prosecution, and she testified on our behalf. She concluded that I wasn't a violent person and testified to the fact that I had at least partly been driven to the attacks by curiosity. Her testimony was brief, but it was important to have a counterweight to Hanny Chung's.

Now it was time to wait for the judge's decision. The last year and a half had been a nightmare for me, one made up of court dates, time in jail, pressure from the RCMP, trouble at school, and being kept away from my best friends. I had now managed to sit through the testimony against me. The only thing left to do was pray for a lenient sentence.

Just as we had done the day I was released from custody after my initial arrest, Yan, my father, and I went to Elio Pizzeria to eat and to discuss my fate. That other meal had been in April 2000, the beginning of this ordeal. Now, just over a year later, we sat and ate, knowing that the end, or at least the beginning of the end, was close at hand.

CHAPTER TWENTY

"This Adolescent Had a Criminal Intent"

"MICHAEL, HURRY UP, we'll be late."

I was in the kitchen eating my breakfast when my father called to me. I was up early that morning, partly because I knew it was the day I would receive my sentence and partly because I hadn't been sleeping well for weeks. The hearings had ended in June and it was now September. The months had passed slowly; it was an agonizing crawl to the final day.

The prosecution had asked that I spend a year in detention for my crimes, a harsh sentence for someone who had entered a guilty plea, had no prior record, and hadn't committed a violent act like murder. The maximum sentence for a young offender in Canada is two years in detention. The government, FBI, and RCMP all wanted to see me sentenced to something close to the maximum. The goal was deterrence. The U.S. president and Attorney General had both spoken out about the need to send a message to any would-be malicious hackers. Canadian authorities wanted to make sure their country wasn't seen as being soft on computer crime.

I thought about this as I ate my breakfast. I knew deep down that I was about to receive a stiff sentence. I also thought about how people's perception of me had changed over the last year and

a half. When the attacks first happened, people speculated that
they were the work of an advanced group of hackers. The stock
market experienced jitters. The U.S. government expressed
concern. When I was named as a suspect and then eventually
arrested, I was seen as a dangerous hacker. But before long that
began to change. I was labelled a "script kiddie," dismissed as not
knowing how to program, and ridiculed as a joke. I had sat silent
as the views of me merged to form a single, widely accepted
narrative: Mafiaboy wasn't a hacker. He was just a kid who knew
how to run DoS tools. A kiddie, a newbie. No experts ever asked
me about what I had done, and all of my files and programs
had been destroyed when I threw my smashed hard drive off
the bridge.

The RCMP had tracked me online for a couple of months
after I learned I was a suspect in the attacks. I was reckless enough
to still use many of the networks I had compromised, but I wasn't
so dumb that I continued to do the exact same things.

In subsequent media reports, one RCMP officer poked fun at
me for having made an error while typing a computer command
early one morning after having been up most of the night.
The RCMP still wanted to make an example out of me, but it
also felt as though they took pleasure in ridiculing me. I had been
told not to say anything. Me, the mouthy kid who had in part
talked his way into trouble, had managed to keep quiet since my
arrest the previous April.

That morning, I felt bitter and kicked around. I had given the
government what it wanted by pleading guilty, yet I felt certain
this capitulation would have little effect on my punishment.
I already felt punished. Since my arrest, my life had been a mess.
The bail conditions kept me from things that mattered most
to me. Frustration with my situation caused me to act out at
school, which in turn landed me in a detention centre for a

couple of weeks. My three best friends were pretty much strangers to me after being separated from me for a year and a half. Now I was waiting to hear what my supposed real punishment was going to be.

I felt sorry for myself, angry with the RCMP and prosecution, and scared of what the judge would decide. I knew it would be bad. Would he give the prosecution the year it asked for? Or opt for Hanny Chung's recommendations?

I got up and grabbed my coat.

THROUGH THE MEDIA GAUNTLET ONE MORE TIME. Press and cameras were waiting for me outside the courthouse. I kept my head down and rushed past everyone. I told myself this would be the last time I'd have to put up with the media attention. This was a huge comfort to me. One more sign that things were finally getting closer to the end.

I had one brief moment of happiness in the courtroom when I thought that I could possibly be released that day. I had already been in detention and dealt with a year and a half of tough bail conditions. Maybe I could receive time served? I thought about it and then quickly swatted the idea away. It was not going to happen.

From my seat at the defence table I turned around to look at my father and mother. Everyone was nervous and praying for a light sentence. Maybe I could be out of custody by Christmas?

The door to the judge's chambers opened and everyone rose. My heart began pumping, palms sweating. It was the first time I had ever felt this way in court. The anticipation was unlike anything I'd ever felt. I wanted to know *right now*.

The judge didn't waste time. He said I would be sentenced to four months for the DoS attacks and another four months for all of the networks I had compromised. Plus one year of probation after that.

"This is a grave matter," the judge said. "This attack weakened the entire electronic communication system. And the motivation was undeniable, this adolescent had a criminal intent."

My defence of conducting "security tests" had failed. The judge also viewed the network breaches as being just as serious as the attacks themselves. Eight months and then probation. I would almost be nineteen by the time I was finally finished with my sentence. In the end, four years of my life would be drastically altered as a result of my crimes.

At the moment he read out the sentence, I slunk down in my chair and wondered why I had pleaded guilty in the first place. This wasn't a lenient sentence. But my anger soon subsided. I knew why I had pleaded guilty. It wasn't to help out the RCMP, prosecutor, or even my family, though they were a big factor. It was because of what I had done. I was busted. I had fucked up. I wasn't the most responsible teenager in the world, but I realized I needed to face the consequences of my actions.

I've always been taught that a man stands up and takes responsibility. He also needs to accept his punishment. I wanted to take my sentence like a man. After all, in terms of the law, I would be one by the time I was finished serving it.

I didn't expect any leniency at this point, but Yan and the prosecution managed to agree that I would be best served by spending my sentence in a group home rather than a detention facility. The judge agreed. I managed to escape Northview for the final time. I was truly grateful for this surprising help.

I expected to be taken away by an officer, but then Hanny Chung appeared before me and told me he would be driving me to the group home. No handcuffs. This was a good sign. He said I could take a few minutes to speak with my family and Yan.

I thanked Yan for what I genuinely felt was a great job on his part. My parents and I hugged and they said it would be okay.

They said the time would pass quickly. I had already done a brief spell at Northview. This would be different. Longer but easier, they said. I wanted to believe it.

I was saying my final goodbyes when I saw Corporal Marc Gosselin approaching me. Every encounter with him had landed me in a detention centre. I didn't want any part of Corporal Gosselin. But he was coming my way and reaching into his pocket.

Jesus, I thought, what now? You got me, leave me the hell alone.

Corporal Gosselin pulled his hand out of his pocket and handed me a piece of paper. His business card. No hard feelings, Michael, he said. Maybe after you serve your sentence and move on you can think about helping us.

The exchange still baffles me to this day. I couldn't believe he handed me a card and spoke about having me work for or help out the RCMP. Of all the people involved in my arrest and prosecution, Corporal Gosselin is the one I have had the hardest time forgiving. I know he was doing his job, but he also saw to it that my father was arrested (the charges were later dropped). He had handcuffed me and marched me out in front of my school, attempted to pressure me during our conversations, and made a point of telling reporters that I was nothing, just a script kiddie. He was the only person for whom it seemed personal. And yet here he was, standing in front of me, trying to make a peace offering. If my skills were so pathetic, why was he here reaching out to me? Why would he want to work with such a no-talent delinquent? It showed me he knew all along I wasn't just some script kiddie, even though that was the story he fed reporters and the judge.

Corporal Gosselin was the last person I wanted to deal with. I looked at him in disbelief, took his card, and walked away. This was one time I'd leave him on my own terms. I walked to Hanny

Chung's car with Corporal Gosselin's card still in my pocket.
I pulled it out, gave it a look, and tore it to pieces. Scraps of the
card scattered on the ground behind me.

I never looked back.

CHAPTER TWENTY-ONE

Final Odyssey

STRANGELY ENOUGH, the moment I began feeling as though my life was returning to normal was when I stood at the corner of Somerled and Cavendish Streets in the Montreal neighbourhood of Notre-Dame-de-Grâce after my sentence was handed down. Hanny Chung drove me from the courthouse to what would be my home for the next eight months. I stood and looked at the building that housed Odyssey, a group home.

Odyssey had no guards or fences. It wasn't a detention centre. The kids who lived there had behavioural issues or problems at home. Some came from abusive situations; others, like me, were sent for rehabilitation. It was like a boarding house for the troubled and unlucky.

Chung took me inside to meet with Henry, the head of the facility. I immediately felt at ease: Henry was delivering good news. He said I would be attending school during the week back on the West Island. I was also allowed to work at the restaurant, though not full-time. And I would be permitted to spend weekends at home after I had served two-thirds of my sentence. But all of these perks were conditional on me respecting Odyssey's rules and conditions.

Odyssey had a 9 P.M. curfew, though I had to be back from school every day by 4:30 P.M. Tardiness would not be tolerated. I was to obey the staff and not get in any trouble at school or the group home. Breaking any rule would mean a trip back to Cité Des Prairies or a similar detention centre, something I wanted to avoid. Henry made sure I understood everything, and I told him he wouldn't have any problems with me.

I was shown to my room, where I sat, alone. Plain and painted white, the room had only a desk, a bed, and a closet. The window didn't have bars on it. I could run if I wanted to, but that would mean a trip to closed custody. Jail. I had no intention of breaking the rules or trying to get away from Odyssey. Soon I'd be spending weekends at home. Then I'd be gone from Odyssey. Eight months. I could handle that.

After a while, I walked around, checking the place out. Odyssey had a washer and dryer in the basement, a kitchen, a living room with a TV, and bathrooms. Everything was basic. I also learned that five or six other kids were staying there. I was surprised to discover that a few of them were girls. Odyssey was co-ed. Dating was forbidden, but it was nice to have girls around. I made friends quickly, and soon everyone knew why I was there. There was no use in hiding it. The other kids were fascinated that articles were still being written about me.

On weekdays I went to Odyssey High School, an unrelated facility on the West Island. When not working or doing homework, I sat around with the other kids, watching TV or smoking cigarettes outside. After curfew, I read books on astronomy and calculus. The lack of a computer made me rediscover my love of reading. The house had a tiny library, but I was lucky to find books that interested me. I also got my hands on a few books about computer programming.

The structure at Odyssey kept everyone in line, including me. While there, I bonded with Mary, one of the staff. She occasionally took me grocery shopping and on other errands. Mary cared about everyone, but I felt we got along especially well. She didn't judge the kids because of why they were there. She just wanted to help. Mary was a mother figure to me while I was separated from my family.

Every night after dinner Mary and I sat together in the TV room and watched *Jeopardy!*. It was our weeknight routine, and something I looked forward to every day. During commercial breaks she often asked me what I wanted to do with my life. Mary wanted me to realize that I had a future waiting for me when I left Odyssey. She also knew I didn't think much of the school I was attending. It wasn't challenging me, so I just did enough to get by and tried to stay out of trouble.

Apart from Mary, I became close with two of the kids at Odyssey, Tanya and Gary. We played board games, listened to music, and watched TV. We also spent a lot of time sitting on the back steps smoking cigarettes and talking. As long as we obeyed the rules, the staff left us alone. It was far less regimented than what I would have experienced in closed custody, and I felt grateful to be in an environment that gave me some semblance of freedom. Of course, I never forgot I was there to serve my sentence.

I realize now that Odyssey had a significant effect on me. I had just enough freedom to deal with my crimes and sentence on my own terms. But Odyssey was also strict enough to show me what life would be like if I didn't change my behaviour. As well, being surrounded by kids who'd been dealt a tough hand by life made me appreciate the advantages I had grown up with. That experience, and my regular discussions with Mary, gave me the resolve to do better for myself when my sentence was finished.

After three months at Odyssey, I was allowed to play basketball at the local YMCA. Gary and I went there whenever we had the chance, and I was grateful to again play a sport that had once been so important to me. I then earned another important privilege when I was allowed to go home on weekends. I was slowly easing back into my old life. Those weekends were filled with friends—though not the three I was still forbidden from seeing—and great food. My family welcomed me home each week as if I'd just returned from a long trip. We ate home-cooked meals and takeout from my favourite restaurants, and friends stopped by the house to hang out. It was a taste of what life would be like if I stayed on course and finished my time at Odyssey without incident.

With less than two months left of my sentence, I began a daily countdown. My release was in May 2002. I marked off each successive day and kept focused on my goal of going home for good. I remember calling my dad a few days before my release and telling him to be there as early as possible on the day of. With my stint at Odyssey ending, I'd have one year of probation. I was thrilled to be moving on with my life.

The day of my release dawned a beautiful spring morning. I woke up early and began double checking my packing; I wanted to leave my white room just as plain as I had found it, as if I'd never been there. My dad arrived at the time we had agreed on. We brought my stuff out to his vehicle, and I ran back inside for one last goodbye. Mary gave me a hug and told me to stay out of trouble. I owe Mary a lot; Odyssey would have been more difficult without her.

My father drove straight to our house, where my brother and stepmother were waiting for me. My room was as I had left it on the previous weekend, but now I was back for good. I rushed to unpack my things and found myself heading down to the basement. There it was, the white box that had been waiting for me for so many years. The PC was turned off, its screen dark. I only had to press a couple of buttons and I could be back online.

I realized I was still drawn to the computer. My probation conditions prevented me from unsupervised computer use but something even more powerful was holding me back: self-control.

I could have called up to my dad to come down and supervise me, but I didn't want to. I could wait.

I looked at the computer for a few seconds longer, then turned around and went back upstairs.

PART 2

Mafiaboy 2.0

CHAPTER TWENTY-TWO

Life, Uploaded

THE CALLS KEPT COMING. Every once in a while, long after my sentence was served, a reporter would call Yan or my father and say it was time for me to tell my side of the story. Ever since my arrest, journalists and security experts had warned the public about the larger security issues raised by my crimes. They still saw me as relevant. They wanted my story. Just as it had seemed all along, my experience was part of a larger narrative about internet security.

"Despite the capture of Mafiaboy, U.S. security experts said they remain concerned about the growing threat of more sophisticated DDoS attacks against the U.S. private sector infrastructure," read one story in *Computerworld* magazine from January 2001. "Experts cautioned that there are thousands of other individuals still active in the hacker community who pose a much greater threat."

Kevin Poulsen, the former hacker turned information-security writer, argued that the authorities shouldn't bother with me. There were much bigger fish to fry. He warned that the online attacks and vulnerabilities would only increase.

"We now know that the Internet wasn't designed to shoulder a new economy, and we'll need some fundamental improvements before a teenager will have any problem clogging up web sites," he wrote in an April 2000 article, "Free Mafiaboy," for the SecurityFocus website. "Our international, coordinated efforts would be better directed at encouraging academia to lock-down its high-bandwidth, low-security networks so they can't be aimed like fire-hoses at innocent media giants in the future."

Like Allan Paller warning the judge that software and hardware vendors need to do more to secure their products out of the box, Poulsen was trying to sound the alarm about the dangers that lay ahead. These dire warnings came frequently from various knowledgeable sources.

The 2001 *Computerworld* article speculated that, "in fact, the prosecution of Mafiaboy could signal the end to DDoS attacks as we now know them.... The next generation of malicious hackers are learning from his sloppiness."

"This was the tip of the iceberg," said one expert quoted in the article, referring to my attacks. My crimes should have been a wake-up call to industry and governments. They could have dedicated themselves to new initiatives aimed at securing the internet for companies, institutions, and the public. But it didn't happen. Instead, today, just as some of these experts warned, we are dealing with malicious hackers who are increasingly advanced and far more dangerous than ever. The result is increased danger to everyone from basic PC users to global corporations and governments. We are living in an age of Mafiaboy 2.0.

ON THE MORNING OF NOVEMBER 28, 2007, an FBI agent accompanied by local police officers knocked on the door of a home in Whitianga, New Zealand. Already, an international investigation into cybercrime had resulted in eight indictments and convictions. That day, the FBI and police believed they were about to apprehend the mastermind of one particularly dangerous online gang. He was Owen Walker, an eighteen-year-old New Zealand man who was known online by the handle "Akill."

The police and FBI agent took Walker into custody and seized his computer equipment so they could examine the hard drives.

They questioned him at a police station, then released him without charges, making a statement to the press about their visit to his home. Although Walker had thus far avoided charges, the raid on his house was about to become the biggest hacker story of recent years.

Martin Kleintjes, head of the New Zealand police's electronic crime centre, said on a radio program that Walker was the "head of an international spybot ring that has infiltrated computers round the world with their malicious software." Other reports described Walker as the ringleader of an international cybercrime group.

The raid on Walker's home made international news. On November 30, it was reported on the BBC's website that "the FBI estimates that 1.3 million computers were under the control of 'Akill' and were used to embezzle millions of dollars." The idea of a teenage cybercrime kingpin was a hot story, and law enforcement alleged that Walker had been part of a group of hackers spread throughout many countries. The group was apparently organized, criminal, and global—not to mention led, at least in part, by an eighteen year old living at home with his parents. Walker and his crew looked like the real deal.

"You come across only one in your career," Kleintjes told *The New Zealand Herald*. Walker was presented as the very worst of the new breed of online criminals.

The story fascinated me. It had echoes of my experience: Walker's young age, the raid at his parents' home, seizing of computers, international headlines, and a litany of accusations levelled against him. There was also a familiar ring to what he was alleged to have done. Walker was accused of writing a malicious software program that enabled him and his crew to compromise more than one million computers on networks all over the world. With these compromised computers (or "zombies") now in their control, they had linked them together in vast networks called botnets. The use of malicious software to build a botnet was reminiscent of what I had done in preparation for Rivolta. But there was something very different about the allegations against Walker.

While I had acted alone and without any specific criminal intent (meaning I wasn't out to extort money or make a profit with my attacks), Walker was presented as the head of a large, profitable, and highly dangerous cybercrime group. Young hackers in various countries had joined forces with the idea of running a criminal enterprise.

In the end, like me, Walker pleaded guilty to six charges "including dishonest use of a computer, damaging a computer system and possessing software for committing crime," according to an April 2008 report by *The New Zealand Herald*.

Walker's crew, more than any I had read about in the years since my crimes, appeared to perfectly encapsulate how malicious hacking and cybercrime had grown and advanced. This was the world of Mafiaboy 2.0: a far more advanced, dangerous, and criminal version of what I had done.

BY THEIR VERY NATURE, hackers push the boundaries of technology. This is as true of the first hackers at MIT as it is of the many hackers who came after them. But hacking is also usually a reflection of the technology available at the time. The model railroad enthusiasts at MIT had to beg and sneak their way onto the university's computers. There were no personal computers then. Society hadn't yet been transformed by the PC and the internet. As a result, their hacks were known only to a small group of model railroad and computer enthusiasts. Computers were scarce, and so, too, were hackers. As computer technology found its way into businesses such as phone companies, we saw the emergence of the phone phreaks.

The dawn of the PC made computers more accessible, and more people became interested in how they worked. That meant more hackers. Hackers went where the technology was. By the 1980s, computers were becoming available to many. It wasn't a coincidence that the first virus hit ARPANET, the project that would become the internet, in 1980. People will always be tempted to throw a monkey wrench into the system.

Computer technology and the internet are now fixtures in businesses and homes. As a result, incidents of malicious hacking are more frequent. More people, companies, and institutions are at risk. Today there are well over one billion internet users worldwide. People access the network at work and at home. They carry smartphones with which they can surf the web and send email. As more and more of our lives is stored on hard drives, cellphones, iPods, USB keys, and other devices, the need for online security becomes increasingly urgent. Unfortunately, average users are unaware of the proper security measures they should take. Many also don't understand the critical flaw at the heart of our connected world: the internet itself.

The internet was never built with security in mind. The ARPA researchers had a specific mandate, and the network they developed was never meant to facilitate and manage the flow of the world's personal, financial, and corporate information. This has led to online vulnerabilities and attacks that today put both the average person and multibillion-dollar businesses at serious risk. The internet is rife with holes, hackers, fraudsters, viruses, spam, and even organized crime.

"Simply put, the Internet has no inherent security architecture— nothing to stop viruses or spam or anything else," asserts a 2005 article by David Talbot in MIT's *Technology Review* magazine titled "The Internet Is Broken." "Protections like firewalls and anti-spam software are add-ons, security patches in a digital arms race."

The article reports the views of David D. Clark, an MIT professor who was instrumental in creating major internet protocols. Talbot offers the analogy that, "for the average user, the Internet these days all too often resembles New York's Times Square in the 1980s. It was exciting and vibrant, but you made sure to keep your head down, lest you be offered drugs, robbed, or harangued by the insane. Times Square has been cleaned up, but the internet keeps getting worse, both at the user's level, and—in the view of Clark and others—deep within its architecture."

We have built our online world on an infrastructure that is insecure at its very core. Yet we continue to push online at a frenetic pace. I don't advocate staying off the internet; the benefits it offers are far too great. But anyone who uses a computer and connects to the internet, whether for personal or professional reasons, should be aware of the risks involved and how they can protect themselves.

Nearly forty years after the internet's invention, many people still don't understand that sending an email is like mailing a postcard: Your message travels from server to server on its way to the delivery point and during the trip can be read or intercepted by people other than the intended recipient. They forget to update their antivirus software or run a firewall to keep out unwanted intrusions. Personal inboxes are clogged with a never-ending stream of spam and phishing messages. A single click of your mouse can invite a hacker or virus onto your system. Home computers and networks are often left completely unsecured.

Carrying around a smartphone filled with sensitive corporate and personal information is akin to walking around with your driver's licence, banking information, and personal data hanging freely from your body. People know to put their wallet in a safe place, but too many of us don't take the same basic level of care with our online information.

I remain enamoured with computers and the internet. Nothing else has ever captivated me so completely or given me so much inspiration. Yet I can't help but be concerned and even shocked at the way the vast majority of internet users ignore security. My story is meant to be a cautionary tale, but the truth is that my crimes, while serious, seem to pale in comparison with the activities now taking place online. I was at the time seen as the incarnation of the reckless teenage hacker who could wreak havoc in our connected world. Technology, and the internet in particular, has advanced at a fast pace since then. So too have the people who seek to exploit it for criminal or malicious reasons.

"Cyber crime is rapidly evolving from the domain of misguided pranksters, to elaborate, profit-driven schemes involving organized crime syndicates that may be based around the block, or halfway around the world," writes Paul Horn, a senior vice-president at IBM Research, in the February 2006 *Business Week* article "It's Time to Arrest Cyber Crime." "It's estimated that 85 percent of malware [malicious code] today is created with profit in mind. The sobering corollary to that statistic: only 5 percent of cyber criminals are caught and prosecuted."

My crimes came at a time when e-commerce was viewed as the great new hope for the global economy. By attacking some of the world's biggest internet companies, I revealed their weaknesses. The result was a massive reaction by the press and law enforcement. There have, of course, been many other serious incidents of criminal hacking since my attacks in 2000, but none seem to have generated the kind of outcry that was directed at me. This isn't because online security has got better. In fact, it's become much worse.

CHAPTER TWENTY-THREE

Hacking for Country, Hacking for Profit

DURING MY EARLY DAYS ON IRC it was clear that hacking was an increasingly global phenomenon. I regularly met people who were in Russia, England, Romania, and other European countries. TNT, the most advanced hacker crew I was a part of, was dominated by Russians. They had the skills and were frequently the most dangerous people on IRC. Today, Russia is considered to be home to some of the most dangerous hackers on the planet.

"Russia has become a leading source of Internet ills, home to legions of high-tech rogues who operate with seeming impunity from the anonymous living rooms of Novosibirsk or the shadowy cybercafes of St. Petersburg," writes Clifford J. Levy in an October 2007 *New York Times* article. "The hackers go by names like ZOMBiE and the Hell Knights Crew, and they inhabit such a robust netherworld that Internet-security firms in places like Silicon Valley have had to acquire an expertise in Russian hacking culture half a world away." Levy goes on to state that "only the United States and China rival Russia in hacker activity," even though the number of internet users in Russia pales in comparison with those in the United States and China.

It's foolish to try to describe hackers as a single, homogenous community. They range from talented computer programmers who build inventive software programs—or their own computers—to people who engage in online pranks, to those who apply their technical prowess for malicious or criminal goals. As I noted in Chapter 6, *hacker* is something of a negative term today. That's unfair. I still view it as a label of respect. Being a hacker doesn't automatically mean you try to break into networks or cause damage. In a lot of ways, the term denotes a level of technical facility and curiosity (though a mistrust or dislike of authority is often implied, too).

The hackers we hear and read about in the media will inevitably be the ones causing trouble. They make for the best headlines. Few care about a group of a people who come together online to collaborate on code or try to devise a software patch for the latest exploit. The community of white hat hackers is largely unknown.

In today's world, there are still people like I was, young computer hackers who get carried away and cause damage just because they see that they can do it. The difference today is that they are far less of a concern than the global hackers who operate with more specific and dangerous goals. Governments, law enforcement, and industry are well aware that the internet is the new frontier of crime, espionage, and political activism.

Two of the most common motivations for today's malicious hackers are political reasons and profit. Both have global implications.

IN 1992, Mike McConnell, a U.S. Navy admiral who had served as General Colin Powell's intelligence officer, became the head of the U.S. National Security Agency. McConnell knew about ARPANET, the network that eventually became the internet, but he never expected to see it become available to the entire world, or that it would become a primary focus for his new job.

"When I went there in '92, the Internet existed—it was called ARPANET—but the World Wide Web did not," he told *The New Yorker* in 2008. "Then the Web made the Internet accessible for everybody. My world exploded."

Information security is now one of the biggest concerns for American intelligence and the U.S. Department of Homeland Security. According to "The Spymaster," a January 2008 article by Lawrence Wright in *The New Yorker,* the Defense Department alone "detects three million unauthorized probes of its computer networks" every day. These probes are from people looking for a way to steal secrets or damage systems. Similarly, the State Department logs 2 million probes per day. (I can recall many times when my scans turned up vulnerable computers on U.S. military and government networks, though I chose not to investigate this further.)

"Sometimes, these turn into full-scale attacks, such as an assault last spring on the Pentagon that required fifteen hundred computers to be taken offline," writes Wright. "In May [2007], the German government discovered that a spyware program had been planted inside government computers in several key ministries, and also in the office of Chancellor Angela Merkel."

Who was to blame for the malicious software on German government computers? According to the Germans, it was Chinese hackers, though the Chinese consulate called the accusation "preposterous."

Information warfare is not new, but the stakes are higher today than ever before. Nations employ their own teams of hackers to try to steal secrets from other countries. Ed Giorgio, a security consultant and former N.S.A. code breaker, told Wright that "there are 40,000 Chinese hackers who are collecting intelligence off U.S. information systems and those of our partners." According to Giorgio, the United States "should never get into a hacking war with the Chinese." Even without all-out war, smaller battles are waged on a daily basis. The cyberspace struggle for secrets and information supremacy takes place largely out of the public eye, but it has an impact on our world.

In 2005 it was revealed that a team of about twenty Chinese hackers dubbed Titan Rain broke into the U.S. Army Aviation and Missile Command and, according to the director of the SANS Institute, a respected security organization, stole "specs for the aviation mission-planning system for Army helicopters, as well as Falconview 3.2, the flight-planning software used by the Army and Air Force." Over the previous couple of years, the group had infiltrated sensitive computer systems at Lockheed Martin and Sandia National Laboratories, a government-owned company that develops technologies used to manage the U.S. nuclear arsenal.

The Washington Post quoted an unnamed U.S. government official as saying, "It's not just the Defense Department but a wide variety of networks that have been hit.... This is an ongoing, organized attempt to siphon off information from our unclassified systems." Another official told *Federal Computer Week* in 2007 that Chinese hackers will "exploit anything and everything."

The question remains as to whether the increase in hacking from China is part of a concerted government effort or if groups such as Titan Rain work alone and then sell the information they collect to the Chinese government. It could be a combination of the two. What's undeniable, however, is that cyber espionage is a serious threat that's only expected to increase. When the SANS Institute named its Top Ten Cyber Security Menaces for 2008, it placed cyber espionage among the top three threats.

"One of the biggest security stories of 2007 was disclosure in Congressional hearings and by senior DoD [Department of Defense] officials of massive penetration of federal agencies and defense contractors and theft of terabytes of data by the Chinese and other nation states," asserted the SANS Institute in its Top Ten listing of "security menaces" to expect in 2008. "In 2008, despite intense scrutiny, these nation-state attacks will expand; more targets and increased sophistication will mean many successes for attackers."

Many former Soviet Bloc countries are also home to hacking groups. They often band together to send a message to rival countries that interfere in state affairs. One notable example came in April 2007 after the Estonian government voted to move a Soviet-era war memorial. The decision angered the country's ethnic Russian population and a riot broke out, during which one person died. The decision also upset the Kremlin, and Vladimir Putin spoke out against it. Then came the hackers.

Estonia, though a small country, is heavily wired. Internet access was even deemed a human right by its parliament. In response to the moving of the memorial, hackers began targeting Estonian websites with denial-of-service attacks. They hit government and political sites for weeks on end. The goal was to disrupt or even cripple the country's web presence.

"It's taken cyberprotest to the next level," Dorothy Denning, a cybersecurity expert at the U.S. Naval Postgraduate School, told CNET News.com, an online technology news site. "It can happen here or to any country where people are unhappy. These were serious attacks which lasted a long time. And it proves you need defenses."

The length and severity of the attacks against Estonian websites help demonstrate how much this activity has evolved. When hackers targeted the NATO website during the bombing campaign in Kosovo in 1999, it was seen as something of a novelty. They had attacked a single website, rather than multiple targets in one country. Since then, the increase in hacker crews and government-sanctioned attacks has raised the threat level of these activities. The attacks are larger, more coordinated, and frequently aimed at stealing classified information.

Of course, not everyone can land a government job as a hacker. The poor economies of many countries often lead malicious hackers to seek ways to earn a profit from their skills. The best way for a talented programmer or hacker to earn a living in a place such as Romania or Russia is to engage in computer crime. It's now easier than ever to get started in a criminal hacking career. Organized cybercrime syndicates are in many ways the new Mafia.

DURING THE COLD WAR, the KGB and East German Stasi put a huge emphasis on recruiting young, impressionable Western students to become spies. Much of the recruiting was done at universities, specifically during student-exchange programs that saw Western students sent behind the Iron Curtain with the goal of fostering greater understanding between the West and the East.

For young American students, the exchanges were a way to see how the other superpower lived. For the Stasi and KGB, according to an October 18, 1990, article by Jamie Dettmer in *Insight on the News* magazine, which did a joint investigation with the BBC, the exchanges "served as a rich source for recruiting American and British students as long-term penetration agents who could be groomed to work their way into government jobs in their own countries—or into other influential spots in journalism, business, higher education (including scientific and technical studies) or the military."

When the Berlin Wall came crashing down, eventually bringing the Soviet Union along with it, these recruiting drives died down. In recent years, however, a new form of recruitment is once again targeting intelligent young university students. This time it's students in Eastern Europe who show promise as computer programmers. Instead of being approached by a foreign intelligence agency, they are being recruited by criminals who offer high pay to join a cybercrime syndicate. The pay is much better than that at a legitimate job and, the recruiters tell them, no one ever gets caught. Their pitch is, unfortunately, largely true.

"In an echo of the KGB tactics employed during the cold war to recruit operatives, organized crime gangs are increasingly using similar tactics to identify and entice bright young net-savvy under-graduates," reads a December 2006 report issued by global internet security company McAfee. "They are adopting KGB-style tactics to recruit high flying IT students and graduates and targeting computer society members, students of specialist computer skills schools and graduates of IT technology courses."

The report, "Organized Crime and the Internet," paints a dark picture of how roving, decentralized cybercrime syndicates are growing and inflicting serious damage on companies, individuals, and the internet as a whole.

"This is certainly not traditional organized crime where the criminals meet in smoky back rooms," Dave Thomas of the FBI Cyber Division is quoted as saying in the McAfee report. "Many of these cybercriminals have never even met face-to-face, but have met online. People are openly recruited on bulletin boards and in online forums where the veil of anonymity makes them fearless to post information."

One reason would-be hackers in Eastern Europe are targeted is because they don't have the job opportunities of computer students in Western countries. "Many of these cybercriminals see the Internet as a job opportunity," says Thomas. "With low employment, they can use their technical skills to feed their family." They also are approached because their location makes it difficult for law enforcement to track down and bring them to justice. They do their work from Eastern Europe, targeting businesses and individuals in other parts of the world. Although the internet makes it possible to attack computers halfway around the world, law enforcement can't arrest somebody online: It needs to deal with warrants, evidence, extradition—challenges that frequently ensure the culprits remain free to continue their work.

As Clifford J. Levy notes in his *New York Times* article on Russian hackers, "The security firms have not received much assistance from the Russian government, which seems to show little interest in a crackdown, as if officials privately take some pleasure in knowing that their compatriots are tormenting millions of people in the West."

Interpol and other agencies are often left without options even when they believe they have tracked down the source of an attack or scam. The feeling of invincibility enjoyed by many cybercrime organizations drives them to attempt even more dangerous illegal gambits.

Some people are naturally drawn to the seedy underbelly of the internet. The sense of power I experienced after seeing what I could do to Yahoo! was overwhelming and, ultimately, addictive. Like me, there are those who want to amass power, to feel the rush. And if they can make thousands or hundreds of thousands of dollars doing it? Well, that's hard to pass up. It's also hard to defend against. Although there are still many examples of solo malicious hackers causing damage, the new phenomenon of organized cybercrime is society's biggest concern.

"There has been a change in the people who attack computer networks, away from the 'bragging hacker' toward those driven by monetary motives," Christopher Painter, deputy chief of the Computer Crimes and Intellectual Property Section at the U.S. Department of Justice, told Reuters in 2006. "There are still instances of these 'lone-gunman' hackers but more and more we are seeing organized criminal groups, groups that are often organized online targeting victims via the Internet."

In 2006, the FBI estimated that computer crime cost the United States $400 billion. Reuters also reported that "in Britain the Department of Trade and Industry said computer crime had risen by 50 percent over the last two years."

In response to that article, on September 19, 2006, Bruce Schneier, one of the world's most respected cybersecurity experts, wrote on his blog at schneier.com that "cyberterrorism gets all the press while cybercrime is the real threat. I don't think this article is fear and hype; it's a real problem."

At a security conference a year earlier, Painter, who had helped prosecute Kevin Mitnick, detailed the efforts of one investigation, named Operation Firewall. The U.S. Secret Service targeted an online forum called Shadowcrew that was, according to SecurityFocus, a "trading floor for an underground economy capable of providing a dizzying array of illicit products and services, from credit card numbers to details on consumers worthy of having their identities' [sic] stolen." (The article was written by Kevin Poulsen, the former high-level hacker who today works as a senior editor for *Wired News*.) Painter said that hackers in different countries were joining together to breach computer systems, steal valuable information such as credit card numbers, and then offer it to the highest bidder.

The Secret Service eventually indicted nineteen men after it busted a leader of the forum and turned him into an informant. There have been other successes. One notable example came in 2000 and involved Michael Bloomberg, founder of the Bloomberg financial information empire and currently the mayor of New York.

On March 24, 2000, Bloomberg received an email message from a man identifying himself as "Alex." The man claimed to have penetrated the company's computer systems and said he was in possession of employee passwords and sensitive corporate information. Alex said he wasn't a criminal but that he wanted to be compensated for revealing the security breach.

"Three days later, a fax machine rang at the Bloomberg offices," reported *The New York Times*. "Streaming out of the machine came computer screen printouts with confidential corporate files, including Mr. Bloomberg's employee photograph, his computer password and his personal credit card numbers. Thus began a cat-and-mouse game pitting the mysterious Alex against Federal Bureau of Investigation agents and Bloomberg employees acting under F.B.I. direction."

Bloomberg was instructed by the FBI to play along with Alex. He agreed to pay US$200,000 in return for Alex's promise that he would reveal how he infiltrated the system and also help the company fix its defences. A meeting with Alex was set for a hotel in London. The two Kazakhstan nationals who showed up for the meeting were arrested and charged with unauthorized computer intrusion and extortion.

This form of cyber-extortion is one of the many scams pursued by cybercrime organizations. They also dabble in credit card fraud, identity theft, spam, malware, and child pornography. The activities have become more advanced thanks to a mixture of technological know-how and some old-school expertise. Lured by the promise of major profit for minor risk, traditional organized crime gangs have moved to get their taste of the cybercrime bonanza. Hacking isn't just for geeks anymore.

As early as 2002, the Computer Emergency Response Team at Carnegie Mellon University warned that organized crime groups, including the Mafia, were beginning to expand into online crime. Its report "Organized Crime and Cyber-Crime: Implications for Business" stated that "the Internet provides both channels and targets for crime and enables them to be exploited for considerable gain with a very low level of risk. For organized crime it is difficult to ask for more."

Since then, traditional organized crime has pushed online at a rapid pace. In 2007, the CEO of security company McAfee declared that cybercrime was now worth US$105 billion globally—more than the illicit drug trade. No wonder the mob and other organizations want in. In many ways, the scams—extortion, fraud, identity theft—remain the same. Organized crime has been involved in those areas for a long time. But it is adapting to a new environment.

The Mafia, for example, has traditionally been involved in gambling, from running illegal card games to helping build Las Vegas. Online gambling is now a huge, albeit somewhat troubled, industry. In 2004, mi2g, a British internet security company, revealed that online gambling websites were the target of an extortion attempt believed to have originated with organized crime gangs.

In October of that year, online gambling companies received threatening emails demanding payment. The threat was an electronic version of the more traditional "pay us or we'll break your legs/burn down your casino." The email message said that any sites refusing to provide payment would face a DDoS attack that would effectively shut down their businesses. Some sites were attacked even before they received the message. Call it a warning shot.

One March 2004 report by TechNewsWorld stated that security experts believed organized crime syndicates were behind the attacks, and that they had teamed up with virus writers to get the job done.

Thomas Patterson, a former partner in Deloitte & Touche's Security Services Group, told TechNewsWorld that "the criminals aren't necessarily the Mafia; some Mid-Eastern and Asian crime gangs are looking to the Internet to use the same old extortion threats," he said. "It's the same old story; just a new place to play."

To launch a massive DDoS attack, send millions of spam messages, or pursue other scams, criminals need to have access to large networks of compromised computers. I am, of course, familiar with this concept. I was able to take out Yahoo! and other websites because I had spent countless hours building my botnets. While I primarily used my networks to engage in battles for IRC channels, I saw first-hand the power of large botnets. Cybercrime syndicates are also well aware of the potential of these networks. Botnets are one of the biggest threats today on the internet—and one of the most powerful cybercrime weapons. As evidenced by the network of more than one million compromised computers that Akill and his colleagues managed to build, the botnets of today are far more advanced and dangerous than the ones I used to perform my attacks.

My primary targets were computers on academic networks. These computers were hooked up to a massive amount of bandwidth. Today, however, with high-speed internet in so many homes and the ever-expanding growth of bandwidth, one needn't go after a university network to build a botnet. The average home PC will work just fine. That's why there's a good chance your computer or that of someone you know is already part of a botnet. You could unwittingly be a cog in the ever-turning wheel of cybercrime.

CHAPTER TWENTY-FOUR

Attack of the Botnets

ONE AFTERNOON IN LATE 2006, Serry Winkler was relaxing on her couch when someone pounded on her front door. Winkler, a political campaign manager in Denver, Colorado, opened the door to find three sheriffs from nearby Boulder dressed in bulletproof vests with their guns drawn. They had a warrant and demanded to be let in. Winkler was shocked and scared. Then she became confused when informed that the warrant was for her computer, an old machine running the outdated Windows 98 software.

After the sheriffs carted off her hard drive, Winkler learned why her computer was of interest. A criminal operating in Russia had infiltrated her PC and placed it under his control using a piece of malicious software. Winkler recalled that she had security software but had disabled it because it slowed down her aging PC. That left the door wide open for the Russian hacker to compromise her computer and add it to his large network of infected machines. Unknown to her, Winkler's PC was part of a botnet made up of compromised zombie computers. The Russian used her machine to make purchases at Sears using a stolen credit card number. Those transactions eventually alerted authorities and led the deputies to her home.

"I'm a middle-aged single woman living here for six years," she told *The New York Times*. "Do I sound like a terrorist?"

No, but she does sound like a typical victim of the growing botnet menace. Once the domain of the hackers who haunted IRC, botnets are cybercriminals' weapon of choice, FBI director Robert Mueller asserted in a November 2007 statement.

"The majority of victims are not even aware that their computer has been compromised or their personal information exploited," said James Finch of the FBI's Cyber Division in a June 2007 FBI press release. "An attacker gains control by infecting the computer with a virus or other malicious code and the computer continues to operate normally."

Damballa, a U.S. company that works to combat "BotArmies," reports that "more than 11 percent of computers connected to the Internet have already been hijacked by malicious programs called bots. As many as 75 percent of enterprise companies are expected to be compromised this year by a bot."

More than 650 million computers are connected to the internet worldwide. The easiest targets for botnets are home computers running Windows that lack up-to-date security protection. In many ways, that means the average internet user.

The goals of malicious hackers have in general shifted away from gaining notoriety and respect within their community and toward earning a profit. This is no more true than with botnets, which have expanded to dangerous proportions. Many security experts warn that law enforcement and security companies are losing the battle against botnets. The robots are winning.

Of all the online security dangers that have gained strength since my crimes of 2000, botnets rank highest. I used them to wage war on IRC and launch my attacks against sites such as Yahoo! and eBay. But that would be child's play for the botnets of today. I compromised hundreds of computers and chained them together into my personal botnets. Today's most dangerous botnets can, as in the case of Akill, approach or exceed the one million computer mark.

"By far the major emerging threats are botnets and we are also seeing more sophisticated malicious code," Robert Burls, a detective constable in the London Metropolitan Police Computer Crime Unit, is reported as saying in the McAfee report on organized cybercrime. "For example, some malware has the ability to deploy keystroke-loggers, harvest stored passwords and take screen captures of infected hosts. These techniques can enable criminals to obtain full identity profiles from victims as well as being able to potentially access their financial and personal data. "The same report notes that botnets are growing at a fast rate and have become the "preferred weapon of choice" for online criminals.

Although the average internet user often finds it hard to believe that a malicious hacker would find anything of interest on his or her home PC, especially when compared with the fat targets offered by major corporations or government agencies, the reality today is that anyone with an internet-connected computer is a potentially lucrative target. Once able to access your hard drive, criminals can install software to steal your online banking password or other sensitive personal information. They can then clean out bank accounts or use stolen credit card numbers to rack up purchases. Your personal computer is also a useful slave. After being linked to a botnet, it can be commanded to join in on a DDoS attack, be used as a conduit for sending spam, or help spread malicious software that infects other PCs and adds them to the botnet.

Finding targets isn't hard. Today's botnet kings (called "botherders") use more advanced versions of the scanning tools I used to locate computers that hadn't been properly protected or patched with security updates. As a 2006 *Washington Post* story explained, these botherders can, with a few keystrokes, add thousands of PCs to their networks and grab a nap while their preferred brand of malicious software is installed and goes to work.

"In the six hours between crashing into bed and rolling out of it, the 21-year-old hacker has broken into nearly 2,000 personal computers around the globe," noted the *Post* article by Brian Krebs, a respected computer security writer. "He slept while software he wrote scoured the Internet for vulnerable computers and infected them with viruses that turned them into slaves."

The hacker in question went by the handle 0x80. He was a high school dropout who said he earned an average of close to $7000 per month herding bots. He claimed to have control of more than thirteen thousand computers in more than twenty countries. Yet 0x80 considered himself to be at the less dangerous end of the botnet scale because he didn't engage in activities such as cyber-extortion.

0x80 earned his money by placing adware, a form of malicious software, on the compromised computers. Once installed, it collected information about users' browsing habits while also subjecting them to an onslaught of pop-up advertisements. He earned a commission for each successful installation. He would also install a worm that could gather valuable information such as passwords and credit card data.

As dangerous as that sounds, 0x80 is somewhat more restrained than other botherders. Think of the cybercrime gangs that targeted online gambling sites in 2004, demanding they pay between US$10,000 and US$50,000 in extortion money to keep their sites safe from botnet attacks. Or Owen Walker, a.k.a Akill.

The raid on Walker's home in late November 2007 was not an isolated event. In June of that year, the FBI revealed the early results of a coordinated effort targeting botherders. Called Operation Bot Roast, it was meant to target and take down some of the more prolific criminals who utilize botnets to earn money and inflict damage.

"Operation Bot Roast was launched because the national security implications of the growing botnet threat are broad," said the June FBI announcement. "The hackers may use the computers themselves, or they may rent out their botnets to the highest bidder. The more computers they control, the more they can charge their clients."

The announcement included the statement that the FBI had so far identified more than one million U.S. computers that had been compromised by botnets. It also named three men who had been charged as a result of Bot Roast. By November, the FBI announced the raid on Walker's home and revealed that three more indictments had been served. Two previously charged men had pleaded guilty, and three men had been sentenced, including two who used a phishing scam to steal millions of dollars from an American bank. The FBI claimed the accused had caused more than US$20 million in losses.

Aside from their names and a brief summary of the charges against them, the FBI announcements included little information about the men caught in the Bot Roast net. *Info World* magazine decided to dig a little deeper. "The motivations of each perpetrator were far richer, and the nature of the crimes more complex, than a simple rundown of their rap sheets could express," wrote Andrew Brandt in a December 2007 article titled "True crime: The botnet barons." The story also revealed the economics of the botnet business, in which millions of email addresses can be spammed for a nominal fee, and networks can be rented out for days or weeks at a time.

Take, for example, the case of Adam Sweaney, a man in his late twenties who pleaded guilty to felony fraud and computer crimes in September 2004. "Sweaney, a 27-year-old computer technician

from Tacoma, Wash., seems to have started out on the side of the
good guys," reported *InfoWorld*. "But at some point, Sweaney
switched allegiances to the Dark Side. From as early as May 2006
and for nearly a year, Sweaney was infecting PCs with Trojan
horses that built a botnet he later used to transmit spam messages
on behalf of others."

When contacted by an undercover agent, Sweaney happily listed
the rate card for his services. If, say, you had some counterfeit Viagra
you wanted to sell via the internet, for $500 Sweaney would
deliver your spam sales pitch to 50 million email addresses.
He guaranteed that 87 percent of the messages would hit the mark
and not bounce back. The undercover agent posing as a would-be
spammer was even given twenty minutes to log on to Sweaney's
botnet to check it out and verify its power. The agent ended up
buying 18 million Hotmail email addresses and another 14 million
Yahoo! addresses. He also bought himself two weeks on the botnet
in order to bombard the lists with spam messages.

Sweaney was soon busted and, to the dismay of the FBI, it was
discovered that he had compromised a computer inside the U.S.
Department of Justice's Antitrust Division. Yes, a U.S. government
computer had been turned into a zombie and used to spam internet
users. But even Sweaney wasn't the worst of the botherders snared
by Bot Roast.

John Schiefer, a Los Angeles man in his twenties, was well known
in the underground botnet community. He went by the handle
"acidstorm." By day, however, Schiefer acted like one of the good
guys. He worked as a consultant helping companies secure their
networks.

"He's the biggest fear," Mark Krause, a U.S. attorney in the
cybercrime and intellectual property section told the Los Angeles
Daily News. Schiefer represented the nightmare scenario of a
trusted insider who uses his knowledge for criminal purposes.

Among his offences, Schiefer was contracted to work for a Dutch company to install adware on people's computers. Instead of gaining permission from users to install the adware, Schiefer infected their PCs with the software and then claimed his twenty-cent commission for each installation. That earned him roughly US$19,000 in two months. It was at the low end of his crimes. At the same time as he was installing the adware, Schiefer implanted other malicious software that could enable identity theft and fraud. After stealing passwords and account details, Schiefer used the information to make online purchases and money transfers from people's PayPal and bank accounts.

In the end, Schiefer is said to have maintained a botnet with more than a quarter of a million compromised computers. He faced a maximum sentence of sixty years and a US$1.75 million fine. He decided to cooperate with authorities in order to lighten his sentence.

One important element to any botnet is the quality of the malware that is installed on a compromised computer. Malware is the malicious software that turns an average PC into a zombie. Believe me, getting onto a PC isn't difficult. The BBC has reported that internet-based attacks on Windows PCs happen as often as every fifteen minutes. Tons of people are out there scanning for vulnerable computers, and they have no shortage of targets. The key for a criminal is what they do once they've gained access. This is where Owen Walker (Akill) appears to have found his niche. A talented programmer, he reportedly produced highly sophisticated malware that gave his crew an edge in the botnet industry. And yes, it is an industry.

"It's alleged the solitary, sensitive teenager—revealed by his mother as having Asperger Syndrome—is the creator of malware considered to be among the most sophisticated seen," reported *The New Zealand Herald*. "Walker's program is alleged to have been used by cybercriminals ranging from vandals and saboteurs to virtual bank robbers in the United States and is part of a Dutch investigation of an adware scam in Europe."

Walker's software is said to have infected more than 1.3 million computers after being downloaded more than 22 million times. Police believe his handiwork was used by botherders around the world to help build their networks and siphon off cash profits through phishing, identity theft, fraud, and other means.

Operation Bot Roast rounded up a handful of botherders but has done little to slow the growth of botnets. Rick Wesson, chief executive of Support Intelligence, a U.S. company that monitors computer security trends, told *The New York Times* in 2007 that his company was tracking two hundred and fifty thousand new botnet infections *per day*.

"We are losing this war badly," he said.

Which is very bad news for you and your PC.

CHAPTER TWENTY-FIVE

What Lurks
Inside Your PC

HELEN BARROW COULDN'T FIGURE OUT where all her personal files had gone.

Barrow, a nurse in Rochdale, England, logged on to her home computer in May 2006 to discover that the folder containing her files had seemingly disappeared. In its place was a new password-protected folder and a text document titled "Instructions [on] how to get your files back."

Barrow opened the text file and, after a while, realized that a virus had found its way onto her PC. Once on her system, it automatically encrypted her "My Documents" folder and sealed it with a thirty-digit password. Her files—nursing coursework, personal letters, family photos—were now locked away. She read the text file's instructions and learned that the only way to receive the password for her documents was to make a purchase from a specific online pharmacy.

Barrow was the victim of ransomware—a malicious program that finds its way onto a PC and engages in an automated ransom scheme. *Spend this much money at this site or you'll never see your files again.* She couldn't understand how someone had managed to find his or her way onto her PC and achieve such potentially disastrous results.

"When I realized what had happened, I just felt sick to the core," she was quoted as saying in a May 2006 article on the BBC's website. "It was a horrible feeling and I thought I was going to lose all of my work. I had lots of family photographs and personal letters on the computer and to think that other people could have been looking at them was awful."

Barrow was smart in that she contacted the local police as well as an IT expert. Many people would have been tempted to simply pay the amount and get their files back. But that's where the second level of the scam would kick in. The online pharmacy—believed to have been located in Russia—would then have her credit card information. That would likely lead to identity theft and, most likely, fraud. This example shows how quickly a single PC breach can open the door to a string of online crimes. A virus leads to an extortion scam, which leads to a purchase at a specific website, which leads to identity theft, which leads to fraud. If the ransomware writer had decided to include some bot code on that particular program, he could have easily added Barrow's computer to a botnet. Then it would be used to help distribute spam and phishing messages.

All this to say that if you don't think a malicious hacker will find anything of interest on the average PC, you're wrong.

In the end, Barrow was lucky. That particular ransomware program had been tracked by the security industry. The IT expert managed to recover many of her files.

As Barrow's experience illustrates, everyone is a target in today's online world. Cybercriminals consciously try to cast as wide a net as possible. The more users they come into contact with, the better chance they have for success. That's why spam now accounts for more than 70 percent of all email messages in the world, and why viruses and malware continue to grow exponentially.

The computer security company McAfee reported in its December 2006 *McAfee Virtual Criminology Report* that by July 2006 its researchers had detected more than 200,000 online threats. "It took 18 years to reach the first 100,000 (in 2004) and only 22 months to double that figure. McAfee's researchers expect it to double yet again in a similar timeframe."

Things are getting worse for three main reasons. First, the internet and related services continue to expand at a fast pace. More users are coming online, and more systems and devices are being connected. Yet the same fundamental security issues remain. We're patching up the internet and using buggy software and services, rather than rebuilding the network's fundamental architecture. Second, users continue to ignore basic online security advice and leave themselves open to a variety of attacks. Finally, things continue to get worse because those first two factors combine to offer a lucrative market for online scams and crimes. There's a lot of money to be earned.

Each new advancement for the average internet user, be it home broadband, wireless networks, email and web browsing on cellphones, or other innovations, also represents an opportunity for the bad guys. I targeted university networks in 2000 (and before that) because they had access to large amounts of bandwidth. The growth of high-speed internet access for home users has put a similar level of bandwidth in many residences. That means home PCs are a more attractive target than ever before, especially because so many users don't keep their antivirus software and operating systems up to date. This is an invitation to malicious hackers, spammers, botherders, fraudsters, and other online criminal elements.

As a result, the average person has no idea of the malicious programs and other dangers that lurk inside his or her PC. Allow me to crack it open for you.

Malware

In the beginning, the computer gods created hardware and software. Hardware constitutes the "hard" parts, such as a hard drive, that make up the physical components of a computer. Software is the programs that run on the hardware. The keyboard you type on is considered hardware (specifically, a "peripheral" because it is something you plug into the computer). Microsoft Word is the software most of us use when typing a text document. But the ware universe has expanded to include malware, the general term for any kind of malicious software program.

In addition to the aforementioned ransomware, there are spyware, adware, and other nasty evolutions. Simply put, all of these bastardized forms of software have one thing in common: They sneak onto your computer and do someone's dirty work. The end result could be stolen passwords or other personal information, a total shutdown of your PC, or a never-ending stream of ads foisted on you when you go online. They range from the annoying to the downright devastating. It's amazing what a little computer code can do.

There's a good chance that you already have some form of malware on your PC. A 2007 study of three hundred thousand PCs by U.K. security vendor Prevx found that 15.6 percent of machines had at least one active spyware or malware program on them. PCs that had no security protection, such as antivirus software, were 60 percent more likely to have malware on the hard drive. A study by PandaLabs found that 23 percent of home PCs had malware on them, and more than 70 percent of corporate networks with more than a hundred workstations were infected.

Malware typically finds its way onto your system via a website, email, or a software application you have installed. There are multiple points of entry, and the number and complexity of attacks is growing. Viruses, one form of malware, often arrive in your inbox attached to an email. Once on your system, they can delete files, corrupt programs, or erase data from the hard drive, among other things.

F-Secure, a computer-security service provider, reported that at the end of 2007 it was receiving seventeen thousand samples of viruses and other malware each day, seven days a week. This required the service to issue updates roughly five times a day to help keep its customers secure. At the beginning of 2007, the company had catalogued a total of two hundred and fifty thousand types of viruses and malware. By the end of the year, the number had doubled.

"It took 20 years to go from the first virus to 250,000, and now we've doubled that amount in one single year," said Mikko Hyppönen, F-Secure's chief research officer in the company's "F-Secure Data Security Wrap-Up" video posted on its website in 2007.

Worms are another common form of malware. These programs aren't satisfied to simply infect your PC. They're designed to replicate and spread as quickly as possible. The biggest worm of 2007 was the Storm worm. In January of that year, people began receiving emails with the subject line "230 dead as storm batters Europe." Included in the message was an attachment titled "video.exe." Many users thought this was footage of a news report about a massive storm in Europe. In fact, thanks to the ".exe" extension on the file, anyone using a computer running Windows who clicked on the attachment would be inviting the worm onto his or her computer. The .exe extension means the file is executable; it's a self-contained program that runs when you double click to open it. This is the worm. Storm was particularly dangerous because it was a hybrid form of malware.

"Although it's most commonly called a worm, Storm is really more: a worm, a Trojan horse and a bot all rolled into one," writes security expert Bruce Schneier in an October 2007 computer-security column for Wired.com. "It's also the most successful example we have of a new breed of worm, and I've seen estimates that between 1 million and 50 million computers have been infected worldwide."

A Trojan horse is a program that conceals its true identity and intentions in order to get on your system. The "video.exe" file was a Trojan. It was used to deliver the worm. Once on your computer, it places your machine under the control of a botnet.

In previous years, a worm or virus had simply earned a measure of fame for its creator. After infecting a machine, the worm would cause that PC to attempt to infect other users by, for example, using a person's email address book to send out copies of itself. But Storm represents a new breed. Its creator's goal was to infiltrate a massive number of PCs and then chain them to a botnet for future use. It was a clever piece of code because Storm would often lay dormant for a period, thus making it difficult for the user to notice a telltale system slowdown. (Worms also typically burrow their way deep inside a PC so as to avoid detection.)

"If it were a disease, it would be ... like syphilis, whose symptoms may be mild or disappear altogether, but which will eventually come back years later and eat your brain," commented Schneier.

Storm had another important characteristic. After antivirus companies spotted it and began using their services to strip the video.exe attachment from emails, Storm adapted. It began sending out emails informing the recipient that a video of him or her was up on YouTube. (Notice the use of social engineering.) A link was included in the message, but instead of taking the recipients to YouTube.com, it brought them to another website where the worm exploited a security hole in web browsers to help implant its code. Worms and viruses used to spread primarily via email. This is still common, but the malware coders have hit on a new tactic:

using websites to infect users. Users need to be more careful than ever before about the websites they visit.

According to the 2007 annual security report issued by MessageLabs, a computer-security company, "2007 saw cyber-criminals changing their tactics and favoring the method of including links to malicious websites hosting the malware code, rather than attaching the malware to the email itself." The company reported that the use of malicious links had increased exponentially in 2007.

One security expert estimates that roughly eight thousand new links containing malicious software go online every day. The makers of web browsers such as Internet Explorer patch security holes in their products, but, as is often the case with software in general, they are usually one step behind the malware makers.

Three other common forms of malware warrant mention. Spyware is just like it sounds—malicious code placed on your computer to spy on your activities. One common form of spyware is known as a "keystroke logger." Although it's commonly used by employers in England and other countries to see what employees are working on during the day, this software can be deployed to capture passwords and other sensitive information. A keystroke logger is fairly straightforward: It logs everything you type. Malware writers use it to steal online banking passwords and credit card numbers. This information is then sold to the highest bidder. In a January 2008 interview with technology news site VNUnet.com, Maksym Schipka, a senior architect at MessageLabs, revealed that malware programs are often sold for about $250, with each new update costing $25. After using a botnet to spread the malware, the criminal can simply wait for the program to begin collecting personal information and other valuable data.

Each complete identity—which includes a name and address, a scan of a passport or driver's licence, and banking information—

sells for roughly $5. Credit card numbers are also affordable: They can be purchased for between 2 and 5 percent of the remaining credit available on the card. The relatively low prices for such valuable information once again illustrates that this is a volume business. In order to make money, the criminals need to gather mass quantities of personal information. Thus, the onslaught of malware.

In addition to personal information, an attractive kind of data is someone's browsing habits. By tracking the websites you visit, marketers can target more relevant advertisements at you. Google has made a lot of money by placing relevant text ads on its webpage after users enter search terms. But other, less scrupulous, operations prefer to simply overwhelm you with ads regardless of what you're doing. They often do this by using adware, malicious software that sneaks onto your system and takes control of your web browser. If you find yourself overwhelmed by pop-up ads or being taken to websites you never clicked on or typed, you probably have adware on your system.

Adware is attractive to criminals because they often earn a commission for each installation. This commission ranges from five to twenty cents or more per infected PC. The more users being bombarded with ads, the more a company can earn from people clicking on them. Adware is often combined with some form of spyware. After all, why earn money only from the installation when you can also grab some credit card numbers?

Adware and spyware can infect a PC to such an extent that they slow it down to the point of making it useless. As a result, some people just give up and buy a new PC. "On a recent Sunday morning when Lew Tucker's Dell desktop computer was overrun by spyware and adware—stealth software that delivers intrusive advertising messages and even gathers data from the user's machine—he did not simply get rid of the offending programs," reported *The New York Times* in 2005. "He threw out the whole computer."

The *Times* article cited a July 2005 survey by the Pew Internet & American Life Project that found that 68 percent of U.S. computer users surveyed had experienced symptoms consistent with the problems caused by spyware or adware. One computer expert warned the *Times* that "the arms race seems to have tilted toward the bad guys." A computer science professor at Yale declared, "Things are spinning out of control."

In the years since the *Times* article was published, things have continued to get worse. One of the reasons for that, of course, is the rise of botnets. This is the final malware of interest. As I noted, botnets are growing at a shocking rate and they are key to helping spread malware. A high percentage of email-borne viruses, worms, spyware, and other malware is distributed via botnets. Botnets themselves rely on malware to grow. The Storm worm of 2007 included bot code in its package to ensure that any infected computer would become a zombie. It's a vicious cycle in that a single infected PC will assist with infecting others, and on it goes. Meanwhile, the average user is left to work on a sluggish, ad-infested PC that could be stealing sensitive financial and personal information while also eating away at itself.

Isn't technology wonderful?

Spam/Phishing

In early 2004, Microsoft founder Bill Gates took the stage for a Q&A at a World Economic Forum event in Davos, Switzerland. Interviewer Charlie Rose fired a variety of questions at Gates, and one response remains famous to this day.

"Two years from now, spam will be solved," Gates said. He then spoke about Microsoft's "magic solution" to the spam problem. This is how CNET News.com described it in January 2004:

"If you receive an e-mail from an old school friend, and you're happy to receive it, the sender doesn't pay. If it's another offer of a porn subscription, you reject it, and the spammer is forced to cough up."

So far, Gates's solution is still just an idea. As for spam? It continues to clog inboxes, fool users, and wreak havoc online. A lot of people say they're too smart to fall for a pitch contained in an email from a stranger. A Nigerian banker who wants to cut you in on $22 million? Someone selling cheap Viagra? Of course you wouldn't fall for that. Yet spam exists only because it works frequently enough to make it profitable. People fall for the Nigerian banker's pitch. They try to get Viagra on the cheap. They buy that penny stock someone tips them off about.

That's why in 2007 spam was declared to have overtaken real, person-to-person email messages on the internet. Research firm IDC predicted that there would be 40 billion spam messages in 2007, roughly enough for six or seven messages for every person on the planet. Of course, not everyone is online; the lucky souls with email accounts have to bear the burden for the entire globe.

Security company PandaLabs concluded in its 2007 annual security report that more than 50 percent of the email home users received in 2007 was spam; in corporate environments, spam accounted for between 80 and 95 percent. The company also traced the origins of spam messages. Once again, Russia is a country of note: It was responsible for 60 percent of spam. Almost a quarter came from the United States, with Turkey (6 percent), Germany (4.7 percent), and the United Kingdom (3 percent) accounting for the other top spam producers.

Like malware, spam is becoming more inventive. Whereas users would at one time receive a text email offering them Viagra or a hot tip on a penny stock, spammers have now upped their game to get around filters. They have moved away from simple text emails to include different types of file attachments that aren't as easily caught and trashed by spam filters. Or they send the message as an image in order to ensure spam filters can't scan the message content for keywords (such as *Viagra).* There's always a new spam technique that can get around filters.

"In 2007 spammers waged stock pump-and-dump campaigns on the public using Adobe Acrobat PDF format files in order to evade traditional defenses," wrote Mark Sunner, the chief security analyst for MessageLabs in a January 2008 article published on iT News, an Australian technology news website. "Later in the year this moved-up a gear by using other file attachment formats, including Microsoft Excel, Word, ZIP and more notably, MP3. The latter example [consisted] of an audio file attachment where the recipient could at last listen to the spam message being relayed to them."

Ah, what joy. Audio spam! Here's a sample audio spam message that MessageLabs intercepted in October 2007 (an estimated 15 million emails were sent for this particular campaign):

> Hello, this is an investor alert ... "Exit Only
> Incorporated" has announced it is ready to launch its new
> 'text4cars.com' website, already a huge success in Canada,
> we are expecting amazing results in the USA.... Go read
> the news and sit on EXTO.... That symbol again is
> EXTO.... Thank you.

It's a classic "pump and dump" stock scam. Except instead of employing a room of touts who call up suckers and try to push the stock, a spammer simply purchased 15 million email addresses and sent them out (likely by renting a botnet) with an audio pitch included. The spammer would make money by purchasing the stock before the mailing and cashing out after people fell for the pitch and started purchasing the stock, thus driving up its price.

The most important thing to understand about spam is that it's a delivery device. Just arriving in your inbox isn't enough. The goal of spam is to get you to take some kind of action. The Storm worm email wanted you to open the attached file. Stock spam wants you to buy the stock. Messages that say you have a secret admirer or an e-card waiting for you want you to click on the link included. Spam on its own is, of course, an annoyance. If you don't have a good filter set up (all web-based email accounts like Hotmail or Gmail have them), you'll spend a good part of your day cleaning out your inbox. That's a waste of time, but it pales in comparison to what happens when you take action. Spammers work hard to play on fears and desires in order to get you to act on their pitch. They also spend a lot of time trying to make spam appear as if it's legitimate. This is where phishing comes in.

In Chapter 5 I detailed the phishing expeditions I went on during my early days on AOL. Back then, it was easy to pretend to be an AOL employee and get people to reveal their account information. Today's phishers have bigger goals. They send out emails that appear to have come from PayPal, a legitimate online payment service, or from various banks. These emails often include the company's or bank's logo and a serious-sounding message urging you to click on a link to verify your account information. Here's an example:

Dear valued PayPal member,

It has come to our attention that your PayPal account information needs to be updated as part of our continuing commitment to protect your account and to reduce the instance of fraud on our website. If you could please take 5–10 minutes out of your online experience and update your personal records you will not run into any future problems with the online service.

However, failure to update your records will result in account suspension. Please update your records on or before January 30, 2008.

Once you have updated your account records, your PayPal session will not be interrupted and will continue as normal.

To update your PayPal records click on the following link: http://www.paypal.com/cgi-bin/webscr?cmd=_login-run

Thank you,
PayPal Customer Center

Note that the link in the email appears to send you to the PayPal site. But this is not the case. The link actually goes to this website: http://atat.ro/u.php?30. The webpage is set up to look like the PayPal webpage. In fact, it's a dummy page whose goal is to capture your PayPal account information. With that in hand, the phisher can clean out your PayPal account and possibly the bank account connected to it. Here's another example; this letter purports to have come from Chase, a financial institution in the United States:

Dear Chase account holder,

Chase is constantly working to ensure security by regularly screening the accounts in our system.

We have recently determined that different computers have tried logging into your Chase account, and multiple password failures were present before the logons. Until we can collect secure information, your access to sensitive account features will be limited. We would like to restore your access as soon as possible, and we apologize for the inconvenience.

Why is my account access limited?

Your account access has been limited for the following reason(s):

January 9, 2008: We have reasons to believe that your account was accessed by a third party. We have limited access to sensitive Chase account features in case your account has been accessed by an unauthorized third party. We understand that having limited access can be an inconvenience, but protecting your account is our primary concern.

To securely confirm your personal information please follow the link bellow:
    http://premierfirenq.com/manual/Chase/Account/security/login.php

Note: If you received this message in your spam/bulk folder, that is because of the restrictions implemented by your Internet Service Provider. We are sorry for that inconvenience.

The note at the bottom is meant to assure anyone who saw the message in his or her spam folder. That single sentence could be the hook that snags a victim.

Like other attacks, phishing scams are on the rise. In December 2007 alone, PhishTank, a clearinghouse that collects suspected phishing emails, processed more than eleven thousand phishing samples. Of those emails, more than four thousand were made to look as if they came from eBay, and more than twenty-five hundred were fake PayPal messages. Other messages purported to come from Citibank, Bank of America Corporation, HSBC, and even the IRS. MessageLabs reports that phishing attacks account for 66 percent of all online attacks, a sharp increase considering that the 2006 average was 34.9 percent.

Part of the reason for the growth of phishing is that, thanks to do-it-yourself phishing kits, almost anyone can get in the game. These kits can be purchased online and are in effect a one-stop shop for any would-be phisher. This means a high level of technical expertise is no longer a prerequisite for launching phishing attacks.

It's rare to see a type of attack become more sophisticated *and* easier to use at the same time. But that appears to be the case with phishing.

One thing that has helped drive phishing's growth is the popularity of instant messaging programs. Many people use Yahoo! Messenger, Google Talk, AOL AIM, or MSN Messenger throughout the day. These applications are increasingly being hit with phishing messages. Gartner Research reports that 2 percent of all internet fraud was initiated by IM messages in 2006. Although still relatively low, IM-based scams are growing at an impressive rate. The Radicati Group, a research firm, estimated that the average IM user is hit with five spam messages per day. The company expected the number to hit twenty-seven messages per day by 2008.

"Cybercriminals that may have used email for their scams are now finding it easier to catch busy IM users off guard and lure them to fraudulent websites designed to steal credit card numbers, login information, social security numbers and other sensitive data," MessageLabs reported in its 2007 annual security report.

The same is true for applications such as Skype, which allows people to make telephone calls and chat over the internet. These voice over internet protocol (VoIP) applications are also being targeted by cybercriminals. The spread of phishing scams to instant messaging and VoIP applications once again proves that any new internet service or application will eventually become a target for the online criminal element. That essential truth also requires me to look beyond the PC when assessing the threats to individual internet users.

In the Cloud

Your data are everywhere. They're held on the servers of the banks and companies you deal with, on government networks and computers, in your web-based email accounts, on the network of the company you work for. If you have a MySpace or Facebook account, then your data are there as well. Use PayPal? More data.

Although personal computers are home to a treasure trove of personal information, today's interconnected world means your life is stored bit by bit on computers in a variety of places. Your life is "in the cloud." The term *in the cloud* refers to cloud computing, having all of your information and applications spread across various servers and web-based services, as opposed to contained on a PC.

A September 2007 article titled "Computer in the Cloud" in *Technology Review* magazine describes cloud computing as "the idea of relying on web-based applications and storing data in the 'cloud' of the Internet." An example of cloud computing is a Hotmail or Gmail account. Your emails are not located on your PC but exist online in the cloud.

The benefit of cloud computing is that you can access your emails or other data anywhere you can get online. Facebook is another example of the cloud. Your profile exists on its servers, not on your PC. That means you can log on to your Facebook profile even if you're over at a friend's house.

Google is one of the leaders in cloud computing. All of its services are run from its massive collection servers that, according to *BusinessWeek's* December 2007 article "Google and the Wisdom of Clouds," are "just out there, somewhere on earth, whirring away in big refrigerated data centers." While Microsoft Word is a piece of software you install on your computer, Google Docs is a web-based service, one that runs over the internet and allows you to write a document from within your web browser.

To access the cloud, you need to be connected to the internet. You also need to be willing to let someone else—a company, an organization—hold on to your data. Cybercriminals know how valuable the data are. They expend a huge amount of energy trying to infiltrate corporate and government networks to get at them. The data on one server could be worth hundreds of thousands or even millions of dollars. And some of that data could be yours.

Cloud computing offers many advantages to internet users. I'm not telling you to stay out of the cloud, only that you need to be aware that it exists, that you are very possibly already in it, and that there are dangers beyond the confines of your home or work PC. Take, for example, social networking websites.

"Cyber criminals are readily plundering the rich plethora of personal information available from social networking sites such as MySpace, Linked-In, Facebook, Plaxo and others to construct a much more personalized style of attack," according to MessageLabs's 2007 annual security report.

Even the cloud is not immune to malware, phishing, and other threats. In fact, it represents the new frontier. For the average user, the key is to recognize the value of your personal information and data and be vigilant about who does and doesn't get it. Admittedly, this can be difficult to do. For example, we can only hope that our government takes the appropriate steps to secure the information it collects in return for certain services. In November 2007, the British revenue and customs ministry admitted it had lost the personal and financial information of 25 million British families.

But sometimes choices can be made when it comes to giving out or withholding data. Doing so in an informed way requires a realization that your information is your property and that it is valuable—both to you and to the legions of online criminals who salivate at the prospect of selling it to the highest bidder.

Whether on a PC or in the cloud, it's essential that we all take the necessary steps to protect our data, and ourselves.

CHAPTER TWENTY-SIX

The Mafiaboy Guide to Protecting Yourself Online

WHEN IT COMES TO INTERNET SECURITY, the most powerful tool isn't a piece of software—it's knowledge. Malicious hackers bank on the fact that you don't know how to protect yourself. With that in mind, I have some basic advice for keeping you and your family from becoming victims.

I hope you now understand the risks out there in the online world and how easy it is for cybercriminals (or, yeah, an out-of-control teenager) to find their way into your life and inflict serious damage. Simply put, you need to take online security seriously. Don't for a second think you aren't a target. You are.

Most people wouldn't dream of leaving their house without locking the doors, yet they routinely leave their PCs wide open to attack. This has to stop. It's only helping make the internet even more insecure and criminalized. I encourage you to start with this basic guide and then dive deeper to learn more from other valuable sources. As the saying goes, knowledge is power. On the internet, it's also protection.

Email Is a Postcard

It has been said many times, but it bears repeating: Sending an email is like sending a postcard. Your message bounces from server to server on its way to the delivery point and can be read or intercepted during this trip. Also remember that even though you delete messages, they will often be held or even archived by your internet service provider (or employer if sent from a company account). Your behaviour online is not inherently private. Always keep this in mind as you type, browse, and chat.

Basic email security requires that you never click on links or files contained in messages from unfamiliar senders, and that you never reply to spam messages. This only serves to tell a spammer that your address is real.

If you feel the need to protect your email communication, there are programs such as Pretty Good Privacy (PGP) that enable you to send encrypted email. (PGP can also be used to encrypt data on your PC.) Unfortunately, many average users find PGP too complicated to use. Take the time to learn how PGP works and also teach those with whom you frequently communicate about confidential or highly personal matters. Sending encrypted email ensures that no one but the intended recipient can read the contents of the message. If your PC is stolen, data protection programs prevent a crook from combing through your email to glean valuable personal information.

Strong Passwords

Amazingly, the most common password used by people online is … *password*. Yes, their password is password. Other popular choices are "123456," "qwerty," "abc123," "letmein," "password1," and the person's first name. Needless to say, these are passwords to avoid. Others to avoid include your birth year, last name, middle name, street name, children's names, or other obvious choices. Weak passwords are an epidemic. People need to stop using them immediately.

There are a few factors to consider when creating a strong password. One is case sensitivity. It is important to mix it up. Making a password *julieb* (all lowercase) would take a hacker a matter of minutes to crack. A password such as *JulieB*, with two capital letters and four lowercase letters, would increase the difficulty of cracking it, though it would still be relatively easy because the password is only six letters long. I suggest a password be a minimum of eight characters, though you should be aiming for nine or more. Then add in non-standard characters such as an exclamation point, ampersand, dollar sign, or the @ symbol. One example would be *JulieB#$%^*. You may be thinking it might be difficult to remember a password like that, but really it isn't. All I did was hold down the shift key and press the 3, 4, 5, and 6 keys after entering "JulieB." If a website prevents you from using these characters, pick a password that contains at least three numbers and try to intersperse them with the letters. An example is "1eg4U2ceeOK."

The final piece of password advice is to keep it private and change it on a regular basis. "Treat your password like your toothbrush," said Clifford Stoll, author of *The Cuckoo's Egg: Tracking a Spy Through the Maze of Computer Espionage*. "Don't let anybody else use it, and get a new one every six months." It's good advice.

Activate and Update Your Antivirus Program

Viruses have plagued the internet from its earliest days as a public network. They are a fact of online life. Antivirus protection is a basic necessity on any internet-connected PC. There are various products out there and they are, for the most part, effective. Some leading products include Kaspersky Anti-Virus, Norton AntiVirus, and—my personal favourite—McAfee VirusScan Plus. I believe McAfee's antivirus service is one of the most advanced, and I have been using it for a long time. The most important thing to remember about antivirus protection is that you must keep it updated. If your service tells you it needs to download an update, do it. Even better, set your preferences so it updates automatically.

Many new computers ship with antivirus software included, but you have to activate it to get it working. Too many people forget this, or don't realize that they will eventually have to upgrade to a paid version. It's worth it. Activate and update. If you can't afford to pay for an antivirus service, try Trend Micro's free virus scan, available at http://housecall.trendmicro.com. Once you see how many viruses are on your computer, you'll probably be motivated to spend the money on a package that runs continuously on your PC.

Use a Firewall

A firewall is essential. Simply put, it keeps people from breaking into your computer, and it can also be effective in defeating Trojans. A lot of users were put off by early firewalls because they were complicated to use. This all changed when Zone Labs created a simple firewall application, ZoneAlarm. The company is now owned by Check Point, but the product is the same. Companies such as McAfee and Symantec (the provider of Norton services) also include firewalls in their internet security bundles—applications that combine antivirus with other kinds of essential protection. The latest versions of the Windows and Mac operating systems also include a basic firewall, so be sure to take the time to learn about them and adjust the settings. A firewall can keep hackers out, scan and remove spyware, and quarantine suspicious email attachments, among other important things. As I say, it's essential.

Update, Update, Update

Whether you run Windows or another operating system, it's essential to install all vendor updates. Because operating systems are large, complicated pieces of software, they inevitably have bugs and holes. These vulnerabilities are discovered by hackers and then used to create exploits. An exploit can, among other things, enable someone to take over your PC and add it to a botnet. Microsoft is constantly issuing patches for Windows in order to plug these holes and eliminate the effectiveness of exploits. As with antivirus software, you absolutely must keep your operating system up-to-date. It is crucial to download system updates. You can set Windows and other systems to do this automatically.

Disconnect When Done

If you have a broadband internet connection at home, there's no need to keep it connected when you aren't online. This is akin to leaving a door unlocked in your house when you go out. Research has shown that an average internet-connected Windows PC can be scanned as often as every fifteen minutes by those looking to find vulnerabilities to exploit. Even though it's easier to leave your internet connection always on, this is an unnecessary risk to take. Every second that your PC is connected to the internet makes it more vulnerable to an attack. Get in the habit of disconnecting, and make it a rule in your house.

Back Up and Compartmentalize Your Data

A general rule for all of your data is that you should always make backups. This is critical because a virus could cause you to lose all your files and other data—a nightmare scenario. But backing up has another advantage: It helps you get in the habit of compartmentalizing your data. There's no need to store *everything* on your PC. If there are sensitive files or other information that you don't need constant access to, save them to an external hard drive or burn them to a CD or DVD. Or use a program such as PGP to encrypt it. This puts the information out of reach if anyone should compromise (or steal) your PC. An added advantage is that your computer will run faster if it's not filled with a ton of information.

Be Obsessive About Your Personal Information

The same principle of compartmentalization holds true for personal information such as your name, address, credit card numbers, and other important details. Don't shop at unfamiliar websites or send your credit card and other information by email. Only provide the minimal amount of information necessary, and be wary of filling out forms on unfamiliar websites. Always remember that your personal information is extremely valuable.

Protect Your Wireless Network

Many people now have a wireless network in their home, but it's shocking how many don't password-protect their network. When setting up your wireless router, create a strong WPA—not a WEP, which is insecure—password for the network *and* the router itself. WPA, which stands for Wi-Fi Protected Access, is a security protocol that encrypts and protects your wireless network. Enabling WPA means people need a password to join your network. Wired Equivalent Privacy, or WEP, is an older protocol that is now too vulnerable to use. All wireless routers ship with WPA installed, but you will need to activate it. Read the instructions that came with the router to find out how.

One mistake many people make is that they create a password for the network and then forget to create a password for the router. Many vendors release routers with a default login and password, or no password at all. This means someone could easily infiltrate to your router, and thus your network. I cannot stress enough the importance of making sure you have a WPA password in place for the network *and* router.

Finally, be sure to change the name, known as the SSID, of your network. The default name will likely be that of the manufacturer of your router, such as "Linksys." Change the name to something that doesn't reveal any personal details. That means avoid calling your network "JohnSmithWireless." Business owners should take particular care to avoid giving their network a name that links it to their company or business operations, such as "DoctorOffice." That's an invitation to malicious hackers looking to steal data or credit card numbers.

For those looking to take their wireless security to a higher level, I suggest you look into learning how to hide your SSID and enable MAC filtering. There are lots of online tutorials for these steps. A basic Google search will bring them to you.

My last, and perhaps most important, piece of wireless security advice is very easy to follow: Avoid open networks and public hotspots. Too many people will blindly join any open network within range, be it in a coffee shop, at the office, or while travelling. If you don't know who's running a given network, you shouldn't join it. Someone can easily set up an open wireless network and then run a variety of attacks against people who join it. This could result in things such as stolen credit card numbers and banking information.

Defeating Spam and Phishing

The most basic way to avoid spam and phishing messages is to use a spam filter. The vast majority of web-based email services, including Gmail and Hotmail, have this built in. They automatically move suspect messages into a separate spam or junk folder. The same is true of desktop email programs such as Outlook, Eudora, and Thunderbird. Enabling a filter will cut down on spam in your inbox. As I previously mentioned, you should never open, reply to, or click on a link or attachment contained in an unfamiliar email.

Spammers realize that many people know these basic rules, and so they do their best to make their messages look as personal as possible. For example, if you have the email address Mike@mafiaboy.com (no, that's not my email address), a spammer's program will send a message that begins "Dear Mike." Don't be drawn in by personalization.

Phishing attacks have also become more targeted and now use email with the recipient's name and email address on the To and Subject lines. So even if your name is correct on an incoming email, you still need to be vigilant.

With phishing, there's one easy rule to keep in mind: Your bank will never send you an email message about your account. (Some will, however, send you email newsletters or other marketing material.) If an email claiming to be from your bank appears to be real, call and check with it. Never, ever click on any links. I also encourage you to consider using an application such as SpoofStick, which helps keep you away from suspect websites. This is useful in the event that you click on a phishing link, as well as for general web browsing.

Use Separate Personal and Professional
Email Addresses

One easy way to cut down on spam is not to publish your personal email address on the internet. Of course, many people have websites, blogs, or other properties that require them to include some form of contact information. If you do need to have an email address published on a webpage, I suggest you create a separate, "public" email account with a service such as Gmail or Hotmail, as both have built-in spam filters to help cut down on incoming messages. Use this account for posting on message boards or filling out online registration forms for websites. Then keep another account for your personal and business correspondence. Spammers have sophisticated ways of harvesting email addresses from the Web. This is one way they build their lists. By separating your public and personal email accounts, you compartmentalize your online identity and help keep spam and phishing messages out of your most important email account.

Plain Text Is Best

Many of today's email programs allow you to send HTML emails. This enables you to format your messages using many of the features offered in word-processing programs such as Word. You can bold, italicize, and use bullets and colours, among other formatting features. Aside from the fact that heavily formatted emails can be hard on the eyes (think of people who use background images or multiple colours in their emails), using and accepting HTML-formatted emails heightens your risk of falling for a spam or phishing scam. Many more advanced email-based attacks use embedded images and links to trick you into thinking they are legitimate. For the sake of security, set your email program to send and receive emails in plain text. This will also prevent you from receiving emails containing malicious code.

Talk to Your Children

Kids can be surprisingly advanced internet users. They are on Facebook or MySpace, use instant messaging and email constantly, and are always surfing to new websites. But just because they know how to use a computer doesn't mean they know how to stay safe online. Train your kids to know all of the above rules. And with kids, the sharing of personal information is even more of a concern. Online predators try to lure kids and teenagers into revealing personal information or into face-to-face meetings. The most important thing for any young person to know is that he or she must never reveal any personal details to strangers or on websites. Even the smallest detail can be used to discern their real identity. I can't emphasize this enough.

If you are worried about your child's online activity, consider installing a keystroke logger. This application captures every keystroke on the keyboard. By going through the logs, you will be able to see what your children are up to and whom they're talking to. I understand that many people—and especially the kids themselves—consider this an invasion of privacy. I offer it as a suggestion; you can make your own decision about it. You can download a free keylogger from www.refog.com.

You probably talk to your kids about being safe when walking the streets or hanging out with friends. Their online activity is no different. The FBI offers a parents' guide for internet safety at www.fbi.gov/publications/pguide/pguidee.htm. Microsoft also offers information about child safety online, at www.microsoft.com/protect/family/guidelines/default.mspx. Educate yourself and then educate your entire family.

One of the maxims of security is that any system is only as strong as its weakest link. I became very good at finding and exploiting that weak link, be it out-of-date software or a misconfigured firewall. There truly is a multitude of ways that a malicious hacker or online predator can find his or her way onto your PC and into your life. Arm yourself with knowledge and the right tools, and you can avoid being yet another victim of our insecure online world.

RIP Mafiaboy

THE DAY MY PROBATION ENDED, I called my friend Brian.

"Holy shit, dude!" yelled the voice on the other end of the line. "Are you allowed to call me?"

"Yeah, bro, it's all good," I said. "I'm in the clear now."

It was May 2003 and my sentence was finished. Eight months in custody and a year of probation. Time served. Done.

I hadn't been allowed to see Brian for just over three years. He was almost as ecstatic as I was. He couldn't believe it was over. I was beaming and laughing into the phone.

Our joy was tempered by Brian telling me that Patrick, another friend I had been prevented from contacting, had got mixed up with some of the wrong people. Brian hadn't seen or spoken to him in a while. Things had changed while I was kept away. This was what I had feared most.

Brian and I made plans to meet at a club later that night. It was a place I had gone to in the past with my brother. The bouncers knew me, as did some of the regulars, but it had been a while since I had been there. With Patrick missing from my old circle of friends, I wondered what else had changed.

At the entrance to the club I was chatting with the bouncers when I felt a tap on my shoulder. I turned to see Brian standing there with a big grin on his face.

"You finally out of the shit?" he said.

We slapped hands and he gave me a shove.

"Good to see you. Now let's celebrate and get a drink on," he said.

We headed for the door, then Brian stopped.

"Actually, wait, this is for you," he said, handing me a cigar.

I had inherited a love of cigars from my father. Brian had remembered and brought me one to celebrate. We held off going inside while I lit the cigar. It was exactly the moment I had been waiting for. I took several puffs and snuffed out the cigar to finish later.

Maybe the club wasn't as packed as I remember. Maybe the music wasn't that good, the women that beautiful, the drinks that cold. But that was how everything seemed at the time. Perfect.

Soon an old acquaintance named Andrea walked over to me and asked where I'd been for so long.

"Some stuff happened." I said. "It's all in the past now."

She pulled me toward the dance floor. I turned to say something to Brian, but he just winked as I disappeared into the crowd.

I was free.

IN THE YEARS SINCE MY RELEASE, and during the year-long probation that followed, I've thought constantly about what I'm going to do with my life. I eased my way back into computers, realizing that my new sense of self-control enables me to experience them in a more appropriate way. I don't engage in online battles or attacks. I don't belong to a hacker crew. Still, I've struggled to find my place with computers. I know the desire and ability to work with them is hard-wired into me, but how do I take advantage of that?

Computers are a huge part of my past; I want them to be part of my future. My time away from a PC and the internet has left me with a lot of catching up to do. I read books and security websites and see how far things have both advanced and deteriorated.

In recent years, I've written a newspaper column about security and worked in a computer store. All along, I've been thinking about my story, trying to come to terms with it. I remain frustrated by the misconceptions about me and still feel bitter about some of things that happened during and after my arrest. I continue to work through those feelings.

What I know for sure is that I want to be one of the good guys helping make the internet more secure. A white hat. I also hope this book helps discourage any would-be malicious hackers from following my path. For anyone considering it, let me say this: It's not worth it.

This book details some of the difficulties law enforcement faces when attempting to track down malicious hackers and online criminals, but the police do have their successes. Think of the amount of jail time given to Kevin Mitnick, Kevin Poulsen, and some of the botherders I've told you about. People do get caught, and the fines and sentences are tougher than ever.

I effectively lost four years of my life because of what I did. I was kept offline and away from my best friends. I was hounded by the press and pursued by the FBI and the RCMP. My crimes caused me to drop out of high school, to spend time in juvenile detention facilities, and to serve eight months in a group home.

Now, more than eight years after the attacks, I finally feel as though I'm getting my life back on track. That's four years of hell and another four to sort it all out. It's not worth it. Once you choose to go outside the bounds of legal hacking activities, you're marked and hunted down. Maybe they won't catch you right way, but you'll forever be looking over your shoulder, forever tainted and held back by your crimes. And if they do catch you, well, prepare for jail because the FBI, RCMP, and agencies such as Interpol love nothing more than to parade and punish their latest hacker conquest.

Maybe that warning won't register with everyone. Let me put it another way. Mark Zuckerberg, the founder of Facebook, got in trouble for hacking into university computer systems while studying at Harvard. He was seemingly at the point where he had to ask himself, "Do I continue down the path of breaking into systems and violating policies, or should I use my computer and programming skills for something more constructive?"

In the end, he decided to work on a social networking site. Facebook is now worth billions. Why choose the other path? It makes no sense to me, especially when your average computer programmer can earn close to or above six figures in the corporate world. That option looks pretty good to me right now.

I think constantly about how far ahead I could be today if I hadn't initiated my attacks in 2000. I would have finished high school, CEGEP, and university. Maybe I would have my own company or be working in the security industry, earning a great salary and challenging myself. Although my actions earned me a measure of fame—which, yes, enabled me to write this book— they haven't made me rich or contributed to my happiness.

I'm now embarking on the next phase of my life and going back to school to gain the knowledge required to work in computer security. By writing the story of Mafiaboy, I'm closing the book on him and moving on for good.

Even though he'll always be a part of me, Mafiaboy is dead. You can call me Michael.

Acknowledgments

My family has given me a huge amount of support over the years. I'd like to thank my dad, mom, Robert, and Carole, as well as my brother, Lorenzo, and sister, Natasha, for all their help and guidance. Marty Belouni, a great friend, has also always been there when I needed him.

Most of all, I want to thank the people who helped make this book possible: Don Sedgwick and Shaun Bradley; Craig Silverman; and Helen Reeves at Penguin Group (Canada).